Sensicle, But Not Always

Brenda Sensicle-Creese

Illustrated by Susan Anderson

authorHOUSE®

AuthorHouse™ UK Ltd.
500 Avebury Boulevard
Central Milton Keynes, MK9 2BE
www.authorhouse.co.uk
Phone: 08001974150

© 2009 Brenda Sensicle-Creese. All rights reserved.

No part of this book may be reproduced, stored in a retrieval system, or transmitted by any means without the written permission of the author.

First published by AuthorHouse 10/8/2009

ISBN: 978-1-4490-2247-1 (sc)

This book is printed on acid-free paper.

Contents

About the Author........................... vii
The Calamitous Cossie........................ 3
The Bash Street Brownie..................... 5
Market Stalls................................ 10
The Lancaster............................... 18
My Elizabeth 21
The Olympic Flame 24
My Special Place............................ 27
The Enchanted Journey...................... 30
My Beloved Country 54
Childhood Memories........................ 56
Racing Pigeon Ring: 65 P 379................ 59
The Return Of Spring....................... 65
The Fenland Highwayman................... 67
The Auction Of Sundries On The Cobblestones... 69
Autumn Aquarelle........................... 72
The Windmill............................... 73
Yesterday 76
The Little Green Bus 80
Beloved Island Home........................ 83
The Bedevilled Moor 84
Down And Out 91
Fisherman's Tale............................ 94
The Candy Floss Caper 105

About the Author

Born in November 1921, at 28 Regent Street, Spalding, Brenda Florence Sensicle spent her formative years exploiting the utter delights of growing up in a small market town on the Fens of South Lincolnshire in the east of England. This at a time when children could safely leave the house after breakfast and not return until tea time, the world was her oyster and she was going to enjoy it!. In 1939, when the war came, things had to change, for Brenda and her many childhood friends it was a tumultuous time, an entirely new kind of adventure. Her war time role, was as an inspector with the Aeronautical Inspection Directorate, conducting final inspections on Lancaster Merlin engine power plants at Rolls Royce. UK based throughout, even in the darkest moments of the war, there where oportunities to travel around England that otherwise she may never have experienced, often either hiking or cycling. After the war, she returned to her home town, where within 5 years she married and began her family of five children. Running a successful grocery shop for 16 years before moving to Whaplode to run a small nursery, growing flowers, another passion of her life. Finally retiring just 2 years ago at age 85 came the opportunity for which her desire to write had yearned.

I was born Brenda Florence Sensicle at 28 Regent Street Spalding, which was near to the Grammar School fields, one of which was covered in buttercups and daises. Here we spent many happy hours making daisy chains. In the next field, there were huge horse chestnut trees, which produced enormous conkers. I can still clearly remember the excitement of gathering them, each one bigger than the last one, and feeling like highly polished mahogany when you took them out of the spiky shell. A deep dyke separated the two fields, from which we used to catch tadpoles with large glass jam jars; we could watch them slowly turn into frogs.

> Gathering conkers, from under the tree,
> Badger, Badger, one, two, three,
> Hide and Seek, skipping, and taking your tea,
> To enjoy a picnic in Ayscoughfee.

2

The Calamitous Cossie.

It was hand knitted, emerald green, with bright yellow dots. The shallow pool at Surfleet Reservoir was the chosen venue for the launching of my exclusively designed spectacular. I struck off boldly, but soon found myself unaccountably labouring, The reason became abundantly clear when I stood up, clad only in two three-foot-long shoulder straps, with two stone of waterlogged cossie round my ankles. With difficulty, I kicked my way to the side and clambered out, only to be faced with the daunting task of escaping unobserved into the bushes.

4

The Bash Street Brownie.

My unending repertoire of bright ideas was at considerable detriment not only to myself, but to any unfortunates presumed guilty by association, being swept along on a tide of enthusiasm. I make no claim to being the founder of dishonourable discharge, but may hold the record for being the youngest. I was sort of drummed out of the Brownies. So it was with a group of unsuspecting little Brownies I encouraged to embark on an adventure, which shall we say was somewhat counterproductive to the teaching of Brownie Laws: *TO DO GOOD DEEDS.* However, one little brownie "blew the gaff", and doubt was cast upon the influence my continued membership might have. So that brief episode in my life passed ignominiously into history.

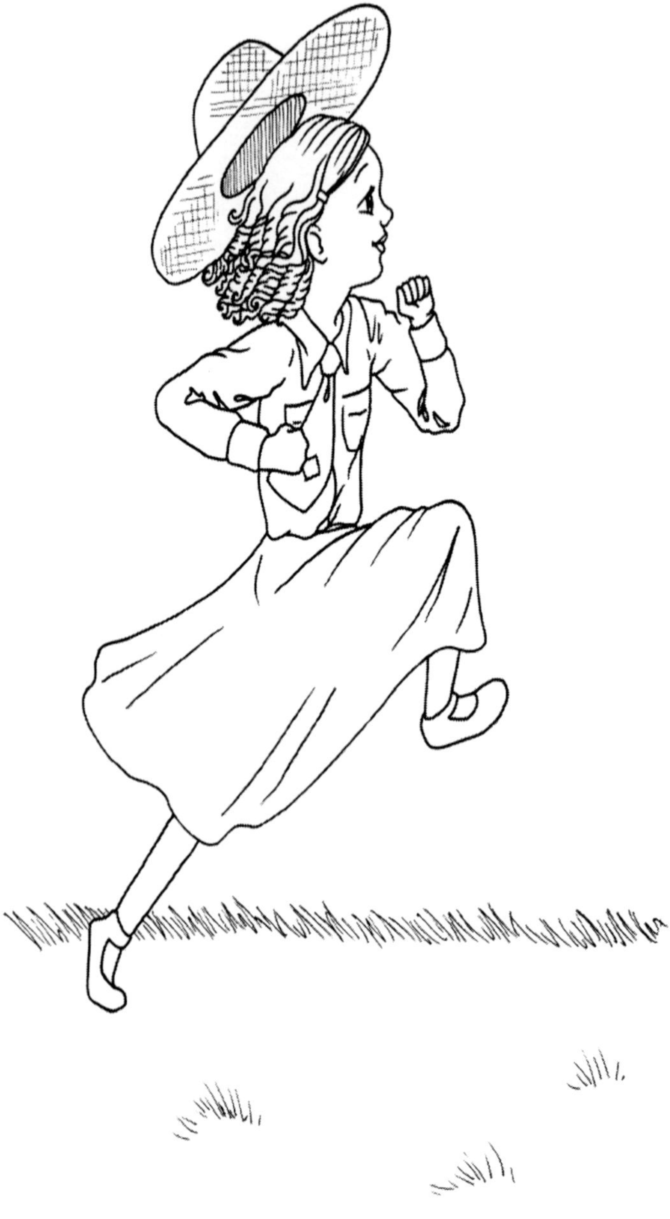

The first thing I really remember is falling down a dyke full of nettles in my Sunday frock, emerging looking like a double helping of sago pudding. The dyke water did nothing for the large ensuing lumps covering all unprotected areas of my tortured body. I remember so well chasing dandelion seed heads in Mr Archer's meadow, believing they were fairies. I can't remember catching any; I wasn't built for speed. The nearest I ever got to being angelic was in a pageant on the vicarage lawn as a fairy, albeit of the somewhat rotund variety.

My next bid for a life, "Treading the Boards", was no more successful. I was intended to be part of a historical tableau at the Church Cote. Unfortunately, I was late on stage. I ran up the steps, also up the front of my crinoline. Unable to stand erect, I rocked to and fro, then toppled slowly over, my face just round the open curtain, hardly, I have to say, in the dignified "enter stage right" tradition.

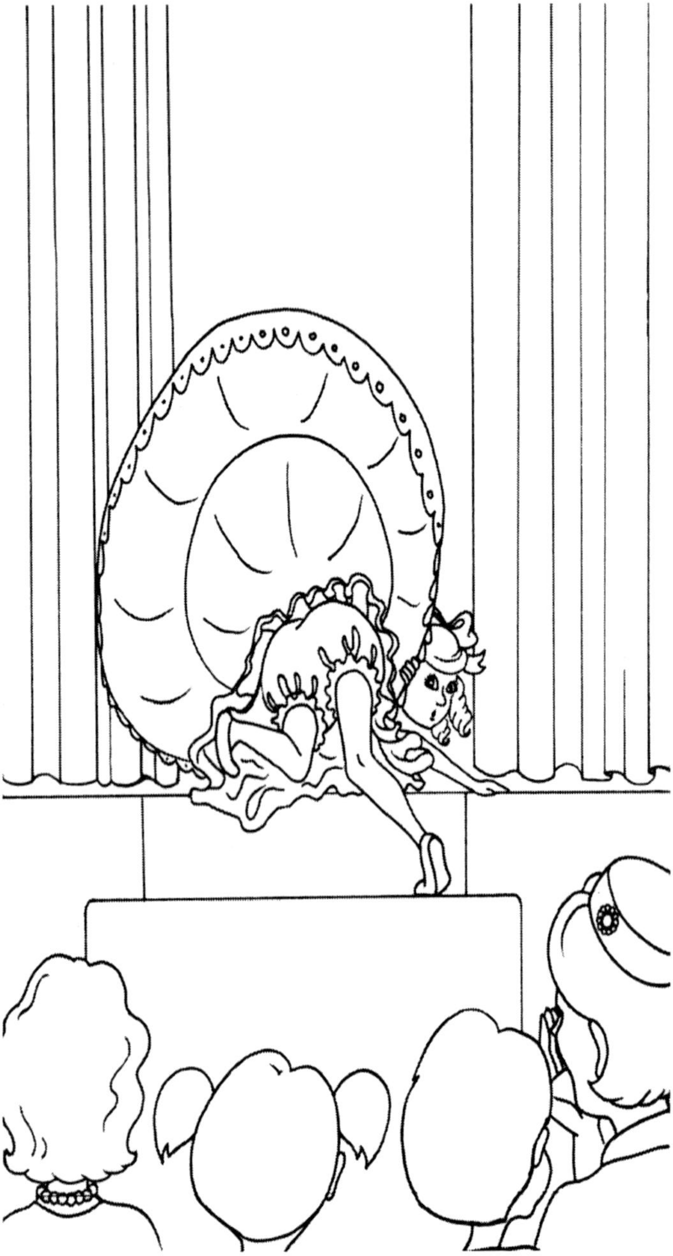

I had started my school years at four and a half years of age, at the Parish Church Day School, connected to the St. Mary and St. Nicholas Church. Consequently, I spent much of my time at church functions, Sunday school, garden fetes, and King's Messengers. The highlights of the year were Prize Giving, Harvest Festival, and the Sunday school outing to Skegness, with free train fare, free lunch and tea in the Pavilion Gardens. My sources of revenue were exploited to the full, in readiness for the big day: that is, running errands, pea pulling and anything else to earn a few coppers. Unfortunately, I always succumbed to travel sickness after a few miles on a train, but it didn't stop me from saving up for the next year. One of my most vivid memories of my early years is going to town with my mother and father on Saturday evenings.\\

Market Stalls.

Wet cobblestones glistened, reflecting bright lights,
From shop windows and stalls, on Saturday nights,
For country town folk 'twas the event of the week,
The cold night seemed warmed, by the bustling street,
The Corn Exchange Clock, with benign expression,
Beamed brightly down on the thronging procession.

Above the Hubbub, loud and clear,
The banter of stall men, shouting their wares,
Instinctively folk are drawn to the sound,
The expectant audience, soon gather round,
At the sweet stall, rows of featureless faces,
Except for the ones that watched and waited,
Huge bags of Bulls eyes, Pear Drops, and Rock,
Humbugs and toffees, Cachous on top,
Ere who'll give me a tanner, a tanner the lot",
Then the motionless figures sprang into life,
Up went the tanners of husband and wife,
They enjoyed the suspense; it was part of the game,
Even though the price, always ended the same,
They knew there was plenty left to be had,
But each one was straining to get the first bag.

Next a stall of bright pots and pans,
The stall man had magical, dexterous hands,
He had a line of plates spinning madly,
On tips of pliable canes,
And with confidence and ability
The stall man then entertains,
To re vitalize flagging momentum,

He constantly runs up and around,
Amazingly, none of the plates seem ever,
To smash, with a crash, to the ground.
Those were the 'Look behind you days',
Tom Mix, Pearl White, and Rin Tin Tin,
When just for a few pence you got in,
To scream and shout, to warn your heroes,
Of impending danger looming,
Until next week, to stay alive,
Untold hazards to survive,
When every boy was Dixie Dean,
When every girl was a Movie queen.
Playing bowling hoops, whips and tops,
Laughing at Buster Keaton and the Keystone Cops.

And so it was, that those young tender years were overtaken by the first of my precious teenage years. This phase did nothing to stem my inexhaustible zest for life, which manifested itself in this memorable episode. A lengthy spell of below-freezing temperatures caused vast areas of floodwater to freeze over on Cowbit Wash. Then the inevitable dash to the lumber cupboard, to rake out old skates and a pair of old shoes to screw them to. Together, the perfect recipe for disaster. Hopefully my ankles were a year stronger, and the possibility of spraining both ankles at the same time slightly less.

However, undaunted and full of hope, I struck off. Determined this year to conquer the frozen waste, I wobbled on to the ice. Inevitably, the first hour produced a catalogue of hilarious disasters, I have to admit, more like the frenzied antics of Buster Keaton than Sonja Henie.

Nevertheless, at the end of the day, with determined perseverance, I managed to stay upright long enough to persuade my father to accompany me to "to see me skate". Although not entirely convinced by my excited assertions that I was a budding Sonja Henie, he allowed me to place him at a strategically suitable distance for me to get up a head of steam for the display.

The look of foreboding on his face turned to absolute terror, as like a frenzied missile, I hurtled ever nearer my defenceless victim, arms flailing, skates akimbo, totally out of control, finally delivering the "coup de main" under both kneecaps, which sent him sailing backwards on his hands and knees. He rose slowly, unhurt, but brought the audition to a dignified close with a very sober, "I think I'll go home now." The apple of his eye was not the flavour of the month, I fear. His immediate departure confirmed beyond doubt that a repeat performance was not a consideration.

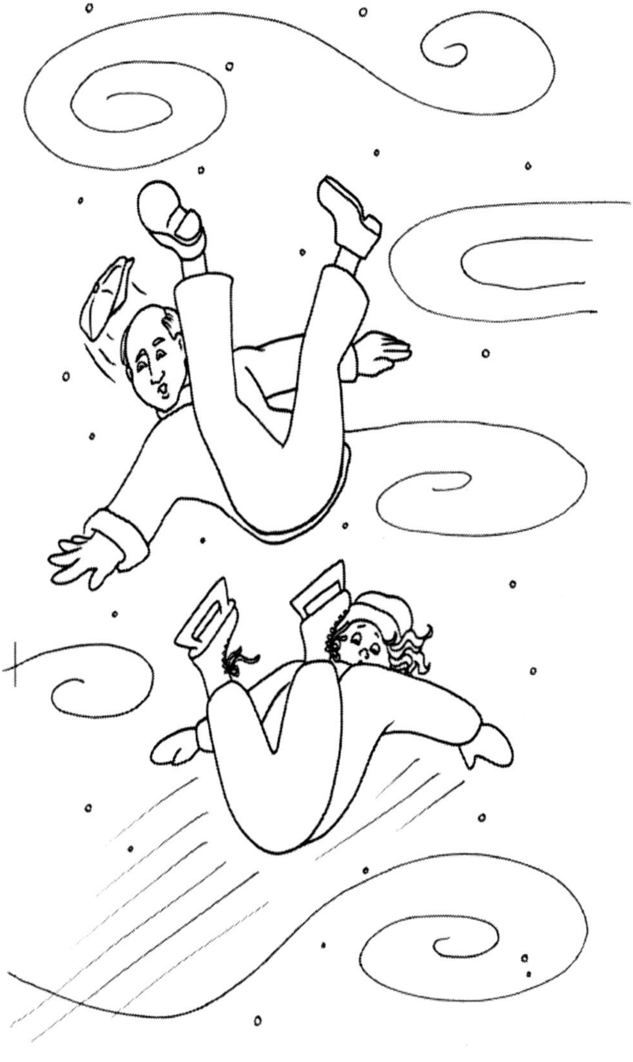

Time inexorably passed, and tender years failed to excuse mad escapades. I left school at fourteen years of age. The regret I felt at leaving was supplanted by the prospect of a new, exciting phase in my life. I started an apprenticeship in drapery, ladies' outfitting, and soft furnishing, I loved it. In those days, a working week in a shop was five and a half days for 5*s* per week for the first year, 7*s* 6*d* for the second year. In return the proprietor had unquestioned loyalty, and strict adherence to the accepted code of courtesy to customers. So much so, that if business was brisk, an air of excitement pervaded the staff, down to the lowliest apprentice, because it mattered; you were part of a team. Looking back, I suppose five and a half days' work for 5*s* sounds a bit like the Queen's shilling, doesn't it? But you didn't mind, because you enjoyed your job. After all, there was still one and a half days and evenings to cram in all the joyous pastimes. There was tennis in Ayscoughee, the Saturday night hop in the Masonic Hall, the midweek dance at the Corn Exchange. A rusty old bike, some emery cloth, and plenty of elbow grease provided my transport for summer Sundays spent in baking sunshine, down Surfleet Reservoir, which was ten to fifteen feet deep in the swimming and diving board area, so you soon learned to swim, or else it was "glug". If finances allowed, you could hire a rowing boat from a weather-beaten old salt for sixpence per person, and the world was your oyster. You could row as far as the Mermaid Inn, if the tide and wind were favourable. The point I am trying to establish is how we tried, and to a great extent succeeded, in making our own amusement. We were so happy, probably because the effort kept us fit and healthy.

In the winter we cycled to the Gliderdrome at Boston on Sundays. Roller skating in the afternoon, dancing in the evening. Life was full of things to do; you were on a roller coaster. The more you did the fitter you got, and the fitter you got, the more you wanted to do, until you felt you could burst with "joie de vivre". There were times when I felt it wasn't fair; I had more than my share. That is the honest truth.

Then came 3 September 1939. I was seventeen years and nine months old when the war began. Some of the local lads had joined the Lincolnshire Territorials the year before. So at nineteen years of age, they were herded into lorries, and whisked off to either RAF Scampton or Waddington, to be placed in embarkation camps, bound for France. Owing to a breakthrough by the Germans, they were forced to retreat to Dunkirk. My brother Jack was one of them. He clambered aboard two small boats; both of them were strafed and sunk. By now almost too tired to care, he climbed aboard a third boat which, thank God, made it back to Britain, and a mug of tea and a wad from the Salvation Army, God bless 'em. Between 27 May and 2 June, 225,000 Brits and 100,000 French and allies were evacuated back to Britain. Every available boat was used, large and small, to ferry the troops. After a spell in Britain, the Lincolnshires were sent on the North African Campaign, and Jack, now a sergeant, whilst on reconnoitre was shell-shocked by mortar bombs. After a considerable spell in hospital, he was given charge of the claims and hirings office in Italy, until the end of hostilities. So he kept his promise, "to do his best", that he made to my father the day they left in the lorries. Such a long time out of a young life.

Back to 1941. At the age of nineteen, I volunteered to go on an engineering course. A most fortunate decision, as it turned out. It was so interesting, that, together with an unexpected aptitude for the subject, it led to a successful placement at Rolls Royce as an examiner in the Aeronautical Inspection Directorate, on Lancaster power plants. The journey to this point was not without its traumas. After cramming solidly almost night and day for six months, sitting exams at two weekly intervals, then came the blow, signing the Official Secrets Act, which stated categorically, minimum age twenty-one years. I was devastated, but clung to a forlorn hope of acceptance, went for an interview, and waited. Then one day a message came for me to go to see a Mr Husbands in the office. This was it. My colleagues wished me luck. Not daring to breathe, I went to the office, frantically searching Mr Husbands's face for some indication if the news was good. He was smiling; I had been accepted. I went, walking on air, to tell my colleagues; I had never felt such elation. Then it was off to Bristol Tech on Prelim Inspection Course for four weeks, back to Rolls Royce for three months' practical, back to Bristol on an aero engineering course for four weeks, and a concentrated series of final examinations. I then went to Rolls Royce Ilkeston for three years, working on Lancaster power plants. Finally I was posted to Hucknall, working on ground position indicators (a bomb-aiming device) and S.P.E. fuel pumps, until the war ended, and with it a never-to-be-forgotten part of my life. After all this, I found it rather difficult to settle down: first in the colliery wages office at Stanton Iron Works, then in pharmaceuticals at Boots Tablet Dispensary. My pastimes during the last two years included being a member of the Youth Hostel Association. I had a group of very good friends, with whom I hiked for miles on hostelling tours, in Derbyshire, Yorkshire, Staffordshire, and North Wales.

The Lancaster.

A symbol of beauty, power, and grace,
With Europe in turmoil,
Fate decreed you must face,
Our need was such, we had to employ,
Such an emotive treasure, to sadly destroy,
To those brave young men, who gave their all, "give thanks"
Now you in quiet repose, so proud you stand, "THE LANC".

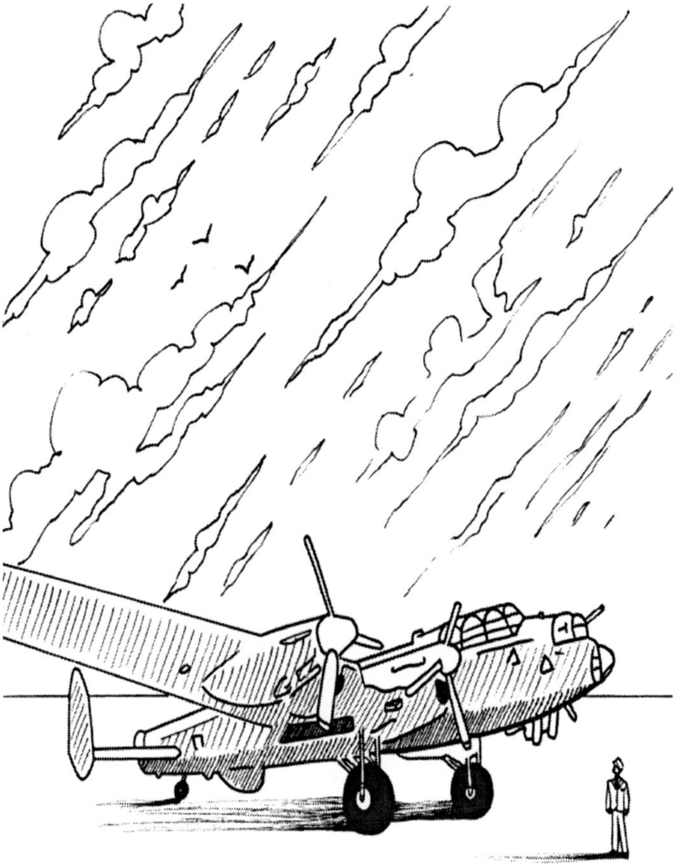

Then I came back to Spalding. I went to work at the Electricity Board Accounts Office, which provided a fantastic sports hall; consequently table tennis became the name of the game. Then it was marriage, and shortly after, I started a business which I ran for thirteen years. During that time we also bred and raced homing pigeons. They are wonderful little creatures.

After that we moved to Whaplode, to a small nursery, an occupation which I found most rewarding, watching those tiny seeds grow into beautiful blooms. That was forty years ago. I called it a day two years ago. Now at eighty-six years of age, this is mainly my occupation, gathering all those memories together, writing about them, and fervently hoping they will stir fond memories with kindred spirits – the old codgers' brigade and all – about when it wasn't all bad, was it? At least you could go into the garden without locking your door. Or let the bairnies out to play with peace of mind. Of course my bairnies are past the going-out-to-play stage: four sons and one daughter, Elizabeth, in whose memory I dedicate this book.

My Elizabeth

You turned, with a smile more golden
than the setting sun that framed you
in the doorway. Silently, the door
closed, upon your smile, the setting sun
and you, my Elizabeth.
Scarlet poppies by the fence, bowed
their heads, to the dove that soared
upwards and onwards, skimming tree and
roof tops. To finally disappear into
the dying rays of the setting sun, as
it slipped silently into evening.

Soon a myriad stars will glisten
In the deep purple night,
Has God in his heaven now,
One more bright star to light.

The days begin and gain their end,
The sun and moon their glory lend,
They pass and merge and change to years,
Each one set, with joy or fears,
But ever in this heart of mine,
The brightest star will always shine,

A love no cloud can ever hide,
Through all the dawns till eventide,
God Bless and keep you ever near,
With our years of memory, ever dear.

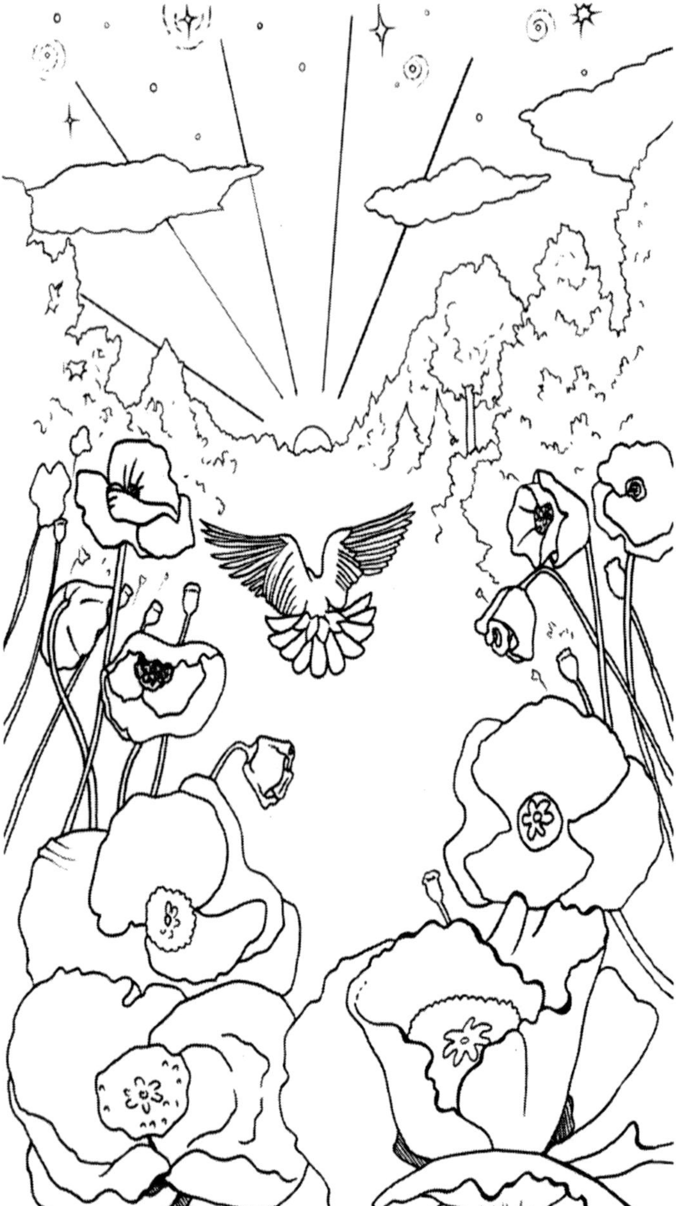

All of them love sport; Elizabeth and Timothy were very actively involved. Both got to English Schools Championships three times, representing their county. They continued to compete as adults and became county champions. Being a decathlete enabled Timothy to amass an incredible haul of gold medals in the County Championships over the years, thirty-six years to be precise. He is fifty years of age now and still competes. Sadly we lost our Elizabeth (Libby) aged thirty-seven from breast cancer. I am proud of my children; they have all done well in their own sphere. Patrick and Johnny organised and funded a junior football team for seven years, "The Young Daniels". Adopting a "no pressure" philosophy, they were very successful, winning many trophies, which included victory in the Manchester United Tournament at Old Trafford. With Robert (Bobby), all the success that he achieves in life will be the result of the abundance of dedicated enthusiasm that he is capable of, with the able support of his wife Hazel, and the love of his children.

> Memories are the shadows,
> that fly the pages of time,
> Perchance to pause in fond recall,
> Such happiness withall.

The Olympic Flame

The contestants geographically,
May live miles apart,
But joy is universal,
To feel it lifts your heart.

In the opening ceremony,
Massive teams march on,
Then from some tiny country,
A lone flag bearing figure,
A total team of 'one',
But this can only,
The Olympic code enhance,
He can still be in there pitching,
and with an equal chance.

The symbol of hope, that unites the world,
To see a nations flag unfurled,
The reward for wearying years of endeavour,
This is a joy, a joy without measure,
Years of striving, ever onwards,
To overcome that barrier of pain,
Yet still have the courage,
To get up! stand tall! and go! and go again!

Not waste God given gift of talent,
Strive on when all energy seems spent,
Fight on, dig deep, and not relent,
How can we not support their dedication,
Or can we deny them that moment of elation,

A moment that is beyond compare,
That we are privileged to share,
When they turn many a joyous tear dimmed eye,
In pride, uplifted to the sky,
To see their nations colours fly,

Since the bygone days of Marathon, Fight on!
For 'twas ever thus,
Not just for themselves, but also,
Carry the baton of hope, 'for us',
To the strains of God Save the Queen, "God BLESS",
To share with her our moments,
Of pride and happiness.

Across the world in friendship
Let us all join hands,
Not just those people near to us,
Also from distant lands
All Gathered in the spirit of that bright Olympic Flame!
Then in full accord and 'one voice' proclaim,
Play up! Play up! and Play the Game.!!

100 M. 400 M. 1,500 M.

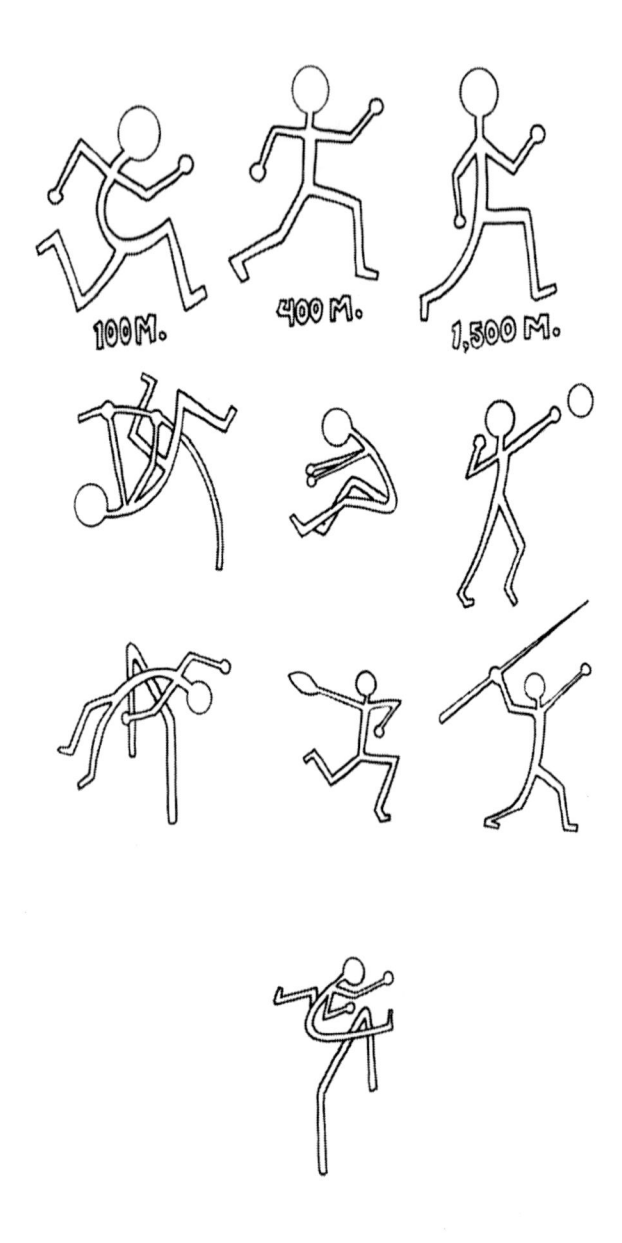

My Special Place

Beneath the trees, wild primrose peep,
Pale hands cupped, to catch the morning dew,
The scent of wild violets, and honeysuckle rose,
Sweet music of bluebells to charm the fairy folk.

'Neath tender leaf and tangled brush,
Where I sought so patiently,
For t'was there I watched the wee folk play,
Now they dance again for me.

We have shared such wondrous secrets,
My memory and I,
Like searching for the crock of gold,
Ending rainbows from the sky.

I found t'was simply just believing,
That turned the golden key,
To a kingdom of enchantment,
'Neath my special wishing tree.

T'was there that I discovered,
The words the song birds sing,
I found the tiny 'music maker',
Who could make the bluebells ring.

He would gather sparkling dew drops,
Then fill each and every one,
With happiness and rainbows,
Mixed with gold dust from the sun.

At sunrise he sprinkled them o'er the glade,
The flowers caught them as they fell,
T'would set the bluebells aringing
Till sweet music filled the dell.

Then, out would come the little folk,
For the new days revelry,
Now as I recall, tis still wonderful,
As they dance again for me.

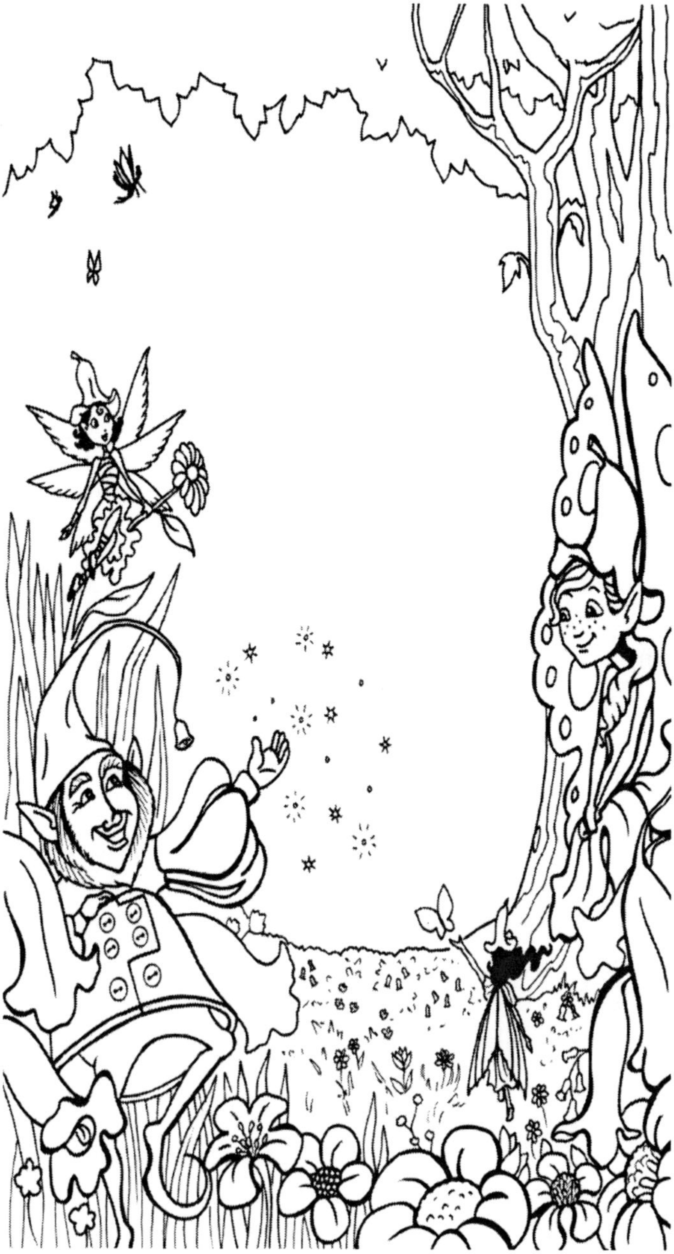

The Enchanted Journey.

The book was lying on the table beside me. From the very beginning, the picture inside had fascinated me, but each and every time afterwards, I was increasingly affected by its strangeness, until in the end, I was almost afraid. Common sense compelled me to look again, to reassure myself that it was just a figment of my imagination. Yet even as I ran my hand over the smooth shining cover, the grotesque little figures that emerged from the garish daubs of colour, were inviting me, or were they daring me, to look again.

I closed my eyes and slowly opened the book. I hardly dared to look, but I had to be sure it was exactly the same as before. The weird absorbing picture, with faces that turned to stare back at me, "the intruder". I watched as the picture slowly started to live; a girl's dress made from paper streamers began to rustle as it was plucked by the breeze. Tiny bells on the gay pointed hats of three quaint little men tinkled as they laughed and danced. The trees of the forest began to gently sway. I could feel the touch of the brushwood upon my legs as I walked towards the girl. My feet crunched in the snow that had fallen between the trees.

The girl seemed to be intently searching for something, when suddenly, she lifted up her hands in joy and amazement, as she saw bright red strawberries peeping out of the snow. The three little men and the girl began to pick them to fill her little basket. "Come and help" called the little men. I stooped to gather the strawberries; I could see now how very beautiful the girl was. "Why do you wear a paper dress?" I asked. "Surely you must be very cold." She replied sadly that her wicked stepmother had sent her into the wood to find strawberries in the snow, clad only in a paper dress, hoping that she would freeze to death and never come home again. Then she told how the kind little men had saved her.

The most amazing thing was as she spoke, a gold coin fell from her lips. Her eyes grew wide with amazement; never had she seen such wealth.

Then quite suddenly through the forest came a handsome young prince. On a splendid white horse. He stopped when he saw the beautiful girl clad only in paper; he pitied her. " Come with me," he said kindly, and helped her on to his horse.

The little men smiled happily; their work was done. I bade them farewell, and set off into the forest. I crossed a small footbridge; I had to stand aside to allow a peculiar string of people to pass. They appeared to be fastened one to the other. "Keep away, for heaven's sake, keep away," they chanted as they disappeared between the trees.

After walking awhile, I came to a clearing, in which stood a tiny cottage. I watched for a moment: an old hag of a woman was trying to persuade the pretty young girl at the window to eat a rosy red apple she held in her hand. "I dare not," the girl replied. "The dwarves told me I must open the door to no one." "You could open the window, that will do no harm," said the old hag slyly. I called out instinctively, to warn the girl. This was met with an instant reaction from the old woman. She swung round in fury. "Don't interfere, you can't alter anything," she spat viciously. At this moment there was an uproarious commotion from the other side of the clearing. A hedgehog riding on a cockerel, driving before him a herd of pigs and donkeys, led the parade, followed by a beautiful maiden hand in hand with a toad, whilst twelve pairs of red shoes danced behind them. Then came a girl in a red cloak, and a wolf who scurried for cover from the woodcutter's axe. Twelve rooks circled above a very handsome, very empty carriage. Overwhelmed in finery, the podgy figure of the old King tottered behind, mumbling, "Off with his head, Off with his head, what's the world coming to, topsy-turvy upside down." The charade ended as suddenly as it had begun.

I found myself standing at the foot of a hill; it was covered in odd black shapes. I climbed to the top, and as I turned, the side of the hill folded back like the leaf of a monstrous book. I could hear the sound of waves breaking on the shore. I walked to the sea's edge, and watched fascinated as the white tips of the waves turned into ice cream cornets. A fisherman was deep in conversation with a fish, whilst his wife sat on a throne two miles high, with three crowns on her head. A faint voice floated down from above, "Get me down, Get me down." I had climbed halfway up, when the icing sugar began to crumble down; down forever I fell.

The fantastic speed with which I was transported from one situation to another, never ceased to amaze me. I surveyed my new surroundings. I appeared to have the choice of two pathways. The one to the right wound slowly up the side of a steep hill, going nowhere in particular; it slowly dwindled away until it disappeared altogether. The path to the left led into dense woodland. I chose the latter. A short distance along the way I came upon a young man who was sound asleep at the foot of a tree, which was laden with golden apples, whilst a golden bird pecked busily away at one of them. My presence in no way disturbed the proceedings, so I turned and made my way into the wood. I was beginning to feel a growing unrest, an urgency, to get away from this ridiculous charade, and these absurd little beings with their nonsensical behaviour.

I travelled deep into the forest, and decided to rest and continue my journey the following day. Alas, this was not to be. I heard the crackling of twigs underfoot as someone approached, and through the trees trotted the panting dishevelled figure of the old King. He hesitated for a moment, then sank wearily down beside me. "I must get back, you know," he confided. "The trial cannot proceed without me." He eyed me up and down. "All persons more than a mile high must leave the court; anyway if I don't get back, we will never know who stole the tarts, and the Queen will be FURIOUS; Off with his head, Off with his head!" His voice trailed away as he gazed miserably at the croquet stick in his right hand, whilst his left hand strived unsuccessfully to control his crown, which insisted on slipping over one eye. "Furthermore," he wailed, "it's my turn to play, and the Queen just beheaded three players who missed their turn." His agitation increased as he envisaged the dire consequences. He removed his oversized crown, and mopped his brow nervously. It was indeed a most handsome crown, made of rich purple velvet, beset with precious stones. His long velvet robe was lavishly trimmed with ermine. I studied the sad podgy figure beside me, with such fine clothes; it was really quite incredible that the result could be so comical. I then explained to him that I could offer no solution to his problem, as I too was lost. He looked more dejected than ever, and we fell silent. By this time darkness had fallen. I felt quite weary; the King was already sound asleep.

In this astonishing world of constant surprises, I expected the unexpected, so when we were rudely awakened by an irritable voice close behind us, I wasn't quite so startled as my newfound companion. "Quite irregular, quite irregular," the voice snapped. I spun around and stared into two large yellow eyes in the upside down face of an owl. With lightning speed he swung round the branch into an upright position. Then clasping his wings tightly behind his back, he took on an air of authority, and looking suitably wise, surveyed us solemnly. He repeated "Quite irregular," Then without any warning, his yellow eyes grew enormous as his face zoomed towards us in a most alarming manner. "Inconsiderate too," he screeched. I fell back aghast, whilst the old king blinked his eyes in amazement. The owl still glared fiercely, but I strongly suspect he was thoroughly enjoying the effect of his outburst. Then puffing out his chest, he began to strut pompously to and fro along the branch. "Now," he said, "about your predicament, twenty leagues from here there lives a wise old man, who has three wise books.

THE BOOK OF LOST PAGES.
THE BOOK OF SORTING THINGS OUT.
THE BOOK OF HAPPY ENDINGS.

"Go to him and ask his help; tell him the upside down owl has sent you, and this," he added with finality, "is all I am prepared to do in the matter!"

When we awoke in the morning, there was no sign of the owl, but I had no wish to renew the acquaintance of the churlish fellow, or his tantrums. We set off at once in the direction that he had vaguely indicated. Our way took us deeper and deeper into the heart of the forest. During this time we came upon a remarkable assortment of people, from peasants to princes, and wizards to witches. Each one was intent on his own business, seemingly quite unaware of our presence. We had no part to play, so we were of no consequence in the order of things. I was however, constantly fascinated by the delightful creatures of the forest, whilst the old King, except for occasionally repeating his conviction, that he was bound to "lose his head", maintained an air of detachment throughout the journey.

We reached the wise man's cottage by nightfall. The King trailed wearily behind me as we approached the tiny door. Recalling our somewhat unfriendly encounter with Mr Owl, I knocked apprehensively. The door opened slowly of its own accord. I peered into the dim untidy little room; the floor was cluttered with jars and pans, books and papers. In the centre a small rocking chair rocked noisily back and forth. It stopped, and the pale blue eyes sitting astride the large purplish nose of the occupant appeared over the top. A mop of spiky grey hair poked out in all directions from underneath a small round black cap.

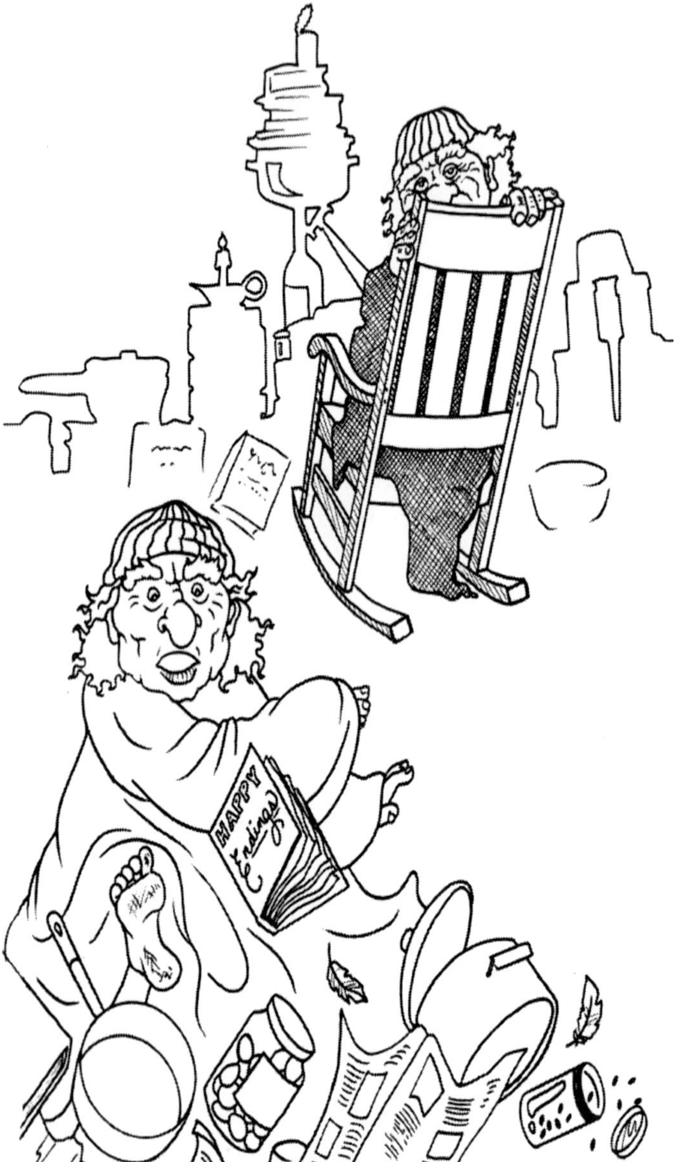
HAPPY
Endings

Obviously more than a little puzzled by our appearance, the wise man stared silently for a moment. Then he leapt from his chair and ploughed jauntily through his disordered possessions towards us. Fumbling into the folks of his long black robe, he produced a ridiculously small pair of spectacles, which he perched on his large bulbous nose, and proceeded to scrutinise us closely.

Without more ado we, or rather I, began to explain our presence, and that we had been directed to him by the upside down owl. "Ah yes," he replied. "An ill-tempered fellow to be sure, but of course we can't change the order of things, it's against the rules you know. If you stay here you're in the way, an encumbrance you understand." He plodded around for some time, hands behind his back, occasionally stopping to survey us with some perplexity over the top of his spectacles, which were now perched precariously on the very tip of his nose; then he resumed his pondering.

The search for a solution was a long and tedious task. *The Book of Sorting Things Out* disclosed nothing, by which time the King was sound asleep, and the wise man was getting a little peevish. He reached for the third and last wise book, *The Book of Happy Endings*. He considered for a moment, then looked under the heading of "Careless Kings and Bothersome Boys." There at long last he found the answer, whereupon he shut the book with such a bang, that the King awoke and jumped three feet into the air. His crown flew off and landed back with such force that his head disappeared inside. He struggled to his feet ready to do battle, blindly brandishing his croquet stick. This vigorous outburst stopped suddenly and he sank exhausted into a corner, uttering muffled wails from inside his crown that the worst had happened, he'd "lost his head". With our combined efforts we managed to pull the crown off again, but still in a state of shock, the King promptly fell off to sleep again.

The wise man bade me to listen attentively. "You have a long, hard task before you," he said gravely. "You must journey through many kingdoms, to the end of somewhere and the beginning of nowhere. You will know this for it will be marked by six black rocks all shaped differently; you will find your answer there. Now you must rest tonight and in the morning I will give you food for the journey, but you must solve the riddles to find the names of wise people from other lands who will help you on your way."

Before we departed in the morning, the wise man gave us the riddle mee rees as he had promised. "But beware," he warned, "when you reach the land of the giants, there is but one there who will help you." Then he handed me a handsome cloth, made from silver thread; in the centre were three golden dragons. "This will supply your needs for the journey," he said. "Guard it well and remember these words:

> On silver threads so pure and fine
> The magic power alone is thine,
> So bring us food and choicest wine.

"And now, my friends, we must say goodbye, and I wish you good fortune." We thanked him for his kindness, and set off in good spirits.

We journeyed through many lands. The magic cloth indeed provided us with most delicious fare, which sustained us throughout our travels. When we were nearing the land of the giants, we stopped to rest one night beside a mountain stream. We had travelled far that day, and were footsore and weary. I sat for a while and watched the water rippling by; it ran shining and crystal clear, except for the angry little peaks of white froth as it strived in vain to dislodge embedded stones; then it swirled and swept on. As I turned away, my royal companion was in the very unkinglike process of plunging his feet into the cool water. The fact that he still wore his stockings and shoes didn't seem to bother him, until one shoe was swept off and went swirling and bobbing downstream, with the King in hot pursuit.

If it hadn't been for the sound of his merry laughter, I wouldn't have noticed the little man sitting on the opposite side of the stream, for he was dressed in green from the toes of his stockings to the tip of his jaunty little hat, from which fluffy white curls billowed round his rosy chubby little face. Still chuckling at the antics of the old King, the little fellow hopped with remarkable agility from rock to rock across the stream towards me. Meanwhile the King was making frantic attempts to rescue the shoe with his croquet stick; he finally succeeded, and came squelching back in his waterlogged shoes. "I've been expecting you," said the little man. I was taken aback for a moment, until I looked again at the wise man's riddle mee rees.

All in green and very small,
At first you think, not there at all,
Not a maid and not a Dame,
You'll chuckle when you hear his name.

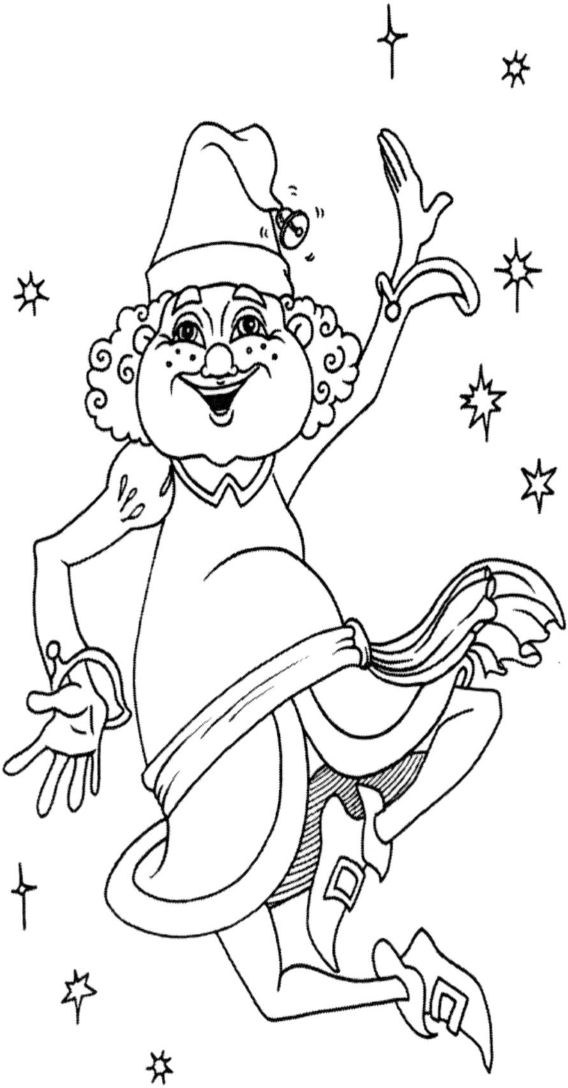

"That's me. That's me," cried the little man excitedly. "I'm Chuckles. Come my friends, follow me, you must take shelter with us tonight." He led us along a narrow pathway to the gate of a beautiful garden; tucked in the corner was the prettiest cottage I had ever seen. As we approached, the door was opened by a white rabbit in a blue gingham apron, with a cap to match perched between two long white ears. "Chuckles dear, where have you been?" she chided, eyeing us with some curiosity. "Look, Matilda, look, I've brought someone to stay!" cried Chuckles excitedly. A dormouse in a tiny lace cap peeped round the door, then a goose in a larger lace cap and a black velvet necklet round her throat. "Come on Tweeny, come on Gani," called Chuckles, "we have some visitors."

For some minutes, Matilda hustled and bustled, Tweeny hurried and scurried, and Gani gobbled and poddled. "I'll get the kettle on for tea," fussed Matilda.

"Please," I said hurriedly, "would you allow us to repay your kindness?" I brought out the magic cloth, and our four little friends gasped in amazement at its beauty. They watched fascinated as I spread it on the table.

> Magic cloth where dragons shine,
> On silver threads so pure and fine
> Bring us food and choicest wine.

There were cries of astonishment; never had they seen such a feast. We all sat down and began to eat heartily. "What a lovely party," twittered the little dormouse, as she munched away, her tiny plate piled high with morsels of delicious cheese and fairy cakes. Everyone was happy;

even the old King entered into the spirit of things. He seemed in a curious sort of way to fit in with the small occupants of the cottage, and certainly found Chuckles a most amusing fellow. It was indeed a most happy party. When we had eaten our fill, we sat down by the window that looked out onto the beautiful garden. In one corner sat an old hen, with twelve golden chicks, which played and nestled under the wings. A Prince and Princess, borne on the back of a winged griffin, came into view. Our little friends rushed to the door. "Good evening, Highness," they chorused. The Prince raised his hand and smiled. "Good evening, subjects," he called, and they sped onwards into the setting sun.

Then quite suddenly the skies became wild and dark with storm clouds. Tweeny covered her eyes. "I hate storms," she twittered tearfully. "Don't be frightened," soothed Chuckles; he took her tiny paw in his hand, and began to dance and jig around the room singing, "We don't care, we are happy and gay, Let the clouds go gathering nuts in May." Then he rocked with laughter, and Tweeny giggled shyly behind her two little paws.

Matilda said, "Really Chuckles, you are a silly goose." At this remark, Gani went bright red with indignation. "Well really, a silly goose indeed, what a cheek," she said angrily, then turned her back and flounced off in a huff. "Oh come on, Gani, Matilda didn't mean your sort of goose," pleaded Chuckles, as he edged alongside and peeped at Gani. Then everyone gathered round anxiously trying to make amends, declaring that far from being a silly goose she was in fact, the cleverest goose they knew. "Yes, and the nicest," piped Tweeny. Gan's shoulders began to shake a little. "I suppose it was just a little bit funny," she giggled tearfully. And all was well once more. I was sorry when the time came to say goodbye to Matilda, Tweeny, and Gani, but with Chuckles for company, the journey to the land of giants was most pleasant. It was here that we regretfully had to part company with the little fellow, and go on by ourselves.

When we had travelled some distance into the land of the giants, we came to the gates of a large, gloomy castle. As we approached, the door opened, and we were confronted by the two largest boots imaginable. I looked up into the red angry face of a giant towering above us. He roared down at us in a most terrifying manner. To escape by running away was impossible. "Come on," I said, grabbing the old King. We dodged smartly between the legs of the giant, into the room beyond. Before the cumbersome fellow could turn around, we had taken refuge behind a huge wooden bedpost, which belonged to an equally large wooden bed. The giant stormed and raged with anger, as he ransacked the room in his efforts to find us. The ground trembled as he stamped around; we stood quaking in our shoes with fright. At long last he appeared to have given up the search. The bed above us suddenly creaked and groaned; indeed it almost descended upon us as the giant collapsed upon it. We waited, hoping he would relax his vigilance. Then above, we heard the sound of snoring, which grew louder and louder, until the windows rattled with the vibration. We crept from our hiding place, and tiptoed to the door. "Make for the caves," I whispered urgently. "Now! Run for it!" In a flash the King swept his robe up over one arm, held his crown on with the other, and bounded off with a remarkable turn of speed. I followed quickly in his wake. He was certainly determined not to be left behind, as his ridiculous figure in bright red pantaloons sped on before me. Even in these terrifying circumstances the sight was absurdly comical. Without slackening our speed, we reached the caves with not a second to spare. A roar of rage from the direction of the castle, told us the giant had discovered our escape. Not until all sounds of him had rumbled away in the distance did we dare to stir from our hiding place. We breathed a sigh of relief at our narrow escape; we really laughed at our predicament. As I looked at the old King's beaming face, I realised that my companion had become my friend, and like me he had adjusted somewhat to our strange surroundings. Moreover, his constant fear of "losing his head", and the queen being "FURIOUS", seemed almost forgotten.

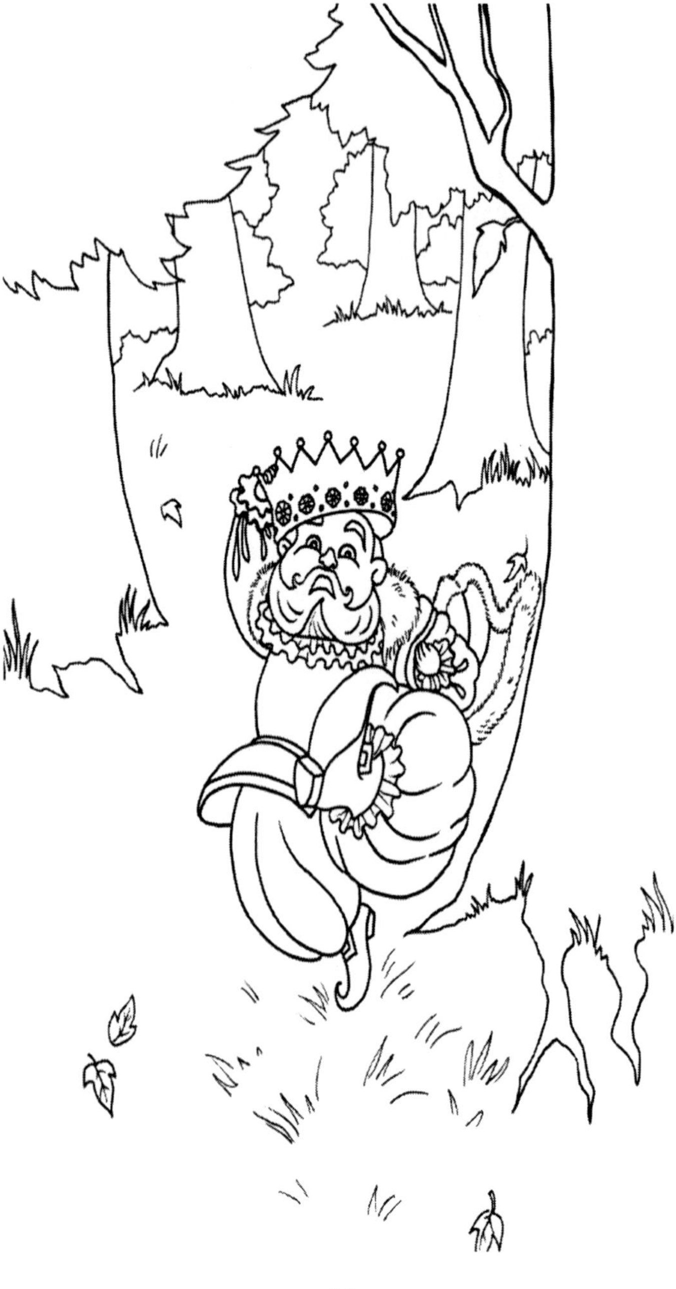

We set off at once at a brisk pace, for should the giant return all would be lost. Taking great care not to make another mistake, we studied the wise man's words carefully. We must journey now to the Great Blue Lake. The last but one of the riddle mee rees ran thus:

> You must keep wide awake, for the fish in the lake
> Perchance you may dream, of a trout in a stream.

After many hours, we came at last to the edge of a lovely blue lake. Clusters of water lilies floated on the surface of water so crystal clear that you could see right to the very bottom. Brightly coloured fish flashed with incredible speed in and out and round about the rocks and stones, then disappeared as if by magic into spiky weeds and water plants that swayed and waved their long leafy fingers in the water below.

At first I thought I had imagined the faint sound of voices and tinkling laughter. I listened carefully. Ah, there it was again. Then I saw them: two tiny people in little green jerkins, and bright yellow hats made from buttercup petals. With peals of laughter they played their game of hide and seek, darting in and out of the snow-white petals of a large water lily. Fascinated, I moved closer; round and round they went. "Oh dear," sighed the water lily, "You're making me quite dizzy." "Don't get fussed, Lily", giggled one little fellow, whilst the other cupped his little hands to his mouth. "Please take us off, Mr Bulrush", he called. The bulrush bent his tall spiked leaves in the breeze; then clinging on, up soared the little people, squealing with delight as they went swinging to the bank. Then they disappeared into the undergrowth.

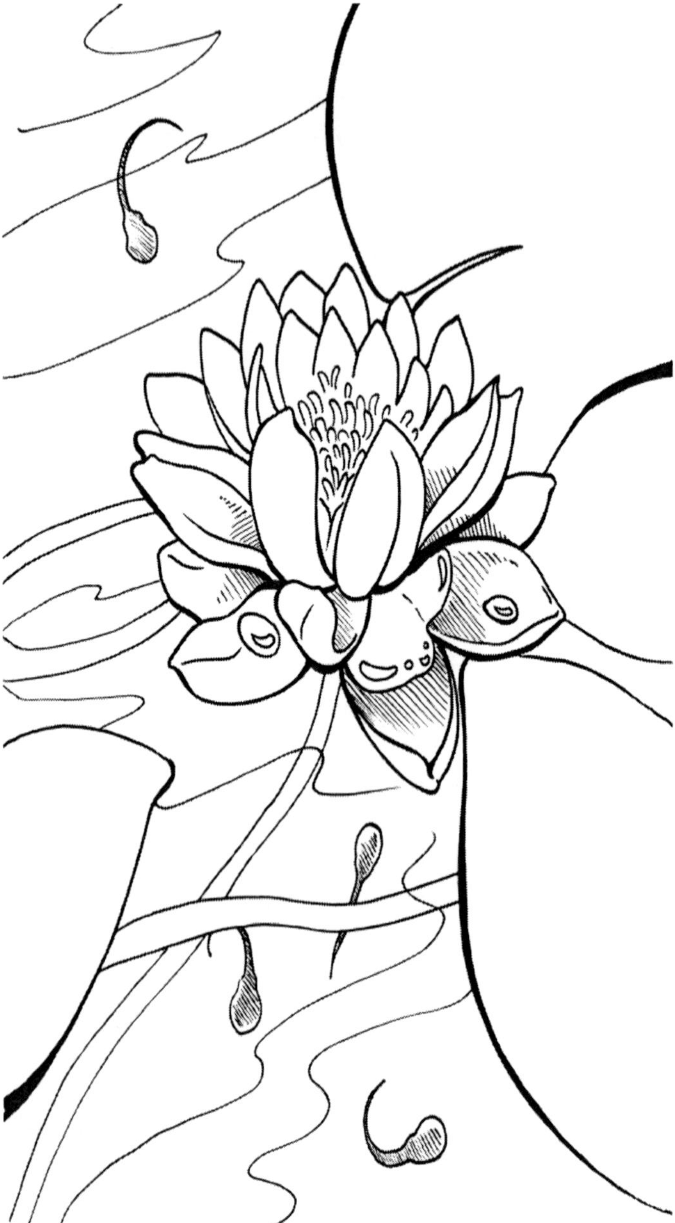

The sides of the lake were surrounded by steep inclines of rocks and boulders, where small rivulets and streams spilled over into the lake below. We found a sheltered spot, and both of us fell fast asleep. I was awakened by a cold flapping and slapping upon my arm. It was a large silvery trout, which had been thrown from the water, and lay stranded upon the bank beside me. I carefully lifted the slippery fellow and put him back into the stream. "Thank you, my friend", he gulped with relief. When he was more composed, he continued, "You must travel northwards, over the Glass Mountain, and there your patience will be rewarded, for you will begin the last stage of your journey". Then with a flick of his silvery tail, he turned and swam swiftly away.

The long climb over the Glass Mountain was indeed most arduous, and we were greatly relieved when the task was over. There was but one more riddle to solve; it ran thus: This is the final riddle mee ree,

> A brave little tailor in the branch of a tree
> Seeking his fortune far and wide,
> Borne along by a giant stride.

The final stage had now been reached, and with growing excitement, we set off in high spirits. We journeyed with little rest for two whole days, but saw nothing and our hopes began to fade. Then we saw them. A huge giant carried a tree across his shoulders, and perched in the branches sat a perky little fellow, singing and whistling as loud as he could. Seeing us approach, the little fellow cried excitedly, "I'm off to seek my fortune." The giant took no notice; he was far too preoccupied carrying the huge tree. "I shall offer my services to the King," the little tailor announced proudly. "Come along my friends, follow us." We followed the strange-looking pair. Even with his heavy burden, the giant set quite a pace.

We came eventually to the gates of a palace. Here the sprightly little fellow leapt down from the tree.

The giant, quite unaware that his passenger had alighted, trundled on. "Now, my friends, I must leave you, for it is here that I seek my fortune," said the tailor. First take heed to what I have to tell you. Not far beyond the end of this kingdom, you will come then to the forest of the mighty winds. He then produced a stone of brilliant colours from a small leather purse about his waist. "This," he said, "will protect you from harm, but you alone must defy the mighty winds, for once you have entered the forest, there can be no turning back. When you reach the end, place the stone at the foot of the tallest oak tree. Then and only then will he let you pass. Once out of the forest, on no account must you turn to look back, or all will be lost." Then the little tailor bade us farewell, and marched boldly through the palace gates.

Following the tailor's instructions carefully, we soon reached the Forest of the Mighty Winds. After his grave warning, we were surprised to find that it appeared quite ordinary. Encouraged by this, we entered boldly, but before we had taken but a few steps, we were assailed by a howling wind, which tore at our clothing and hair with such fury that we clung to each other quite breathless. I took the old King's arm, and together we forged slowly ahead, against a wind enraged with anger at our intrusion. Brown branches, gnarled and leafless, stabbed and poked toward us like long crooked fingers, defying us to go further. The gorse and brushwood hissed with anger; as it snatched and tore at our legs. Our strength was almost spent, when the wind with vicious ferocity screamed in a last desperate attempt to have its way. We clung to each other, unable to move. A few feet away stood the huge oak tree, its thick branches barring the path before us. We lay flat upon the ground and inched our way slowly to the foot of the tree. There I placed the coloured stone. The branches of the oak tree lifted; our way was open. At this very moment the wind ceased to blow so suddenly that we staggered, bewildered and exhausted, into the clearing beyond.

It was exactly as the wise man had promised, the end of nowhere and the beginning of somewhere, and there were the six black rocks, all shaped differently, one of which would hold the key, the answer to everything. The rocks stood side by side in groups of three. We could find nothing unusual in the first group, but the last rock of all turned out to be the entrance to a dark bottomless cavern. Rough-hewn steps in the rock descended down and down into the blackness below. The King peered fearfully down into the darkness, and not wishing to reveal my own anxiety, I tried to reassure him. "Come, my friend, I will lead the way. All will be well." Then I stepped boldly on to the rock and started the descent, and the King followed cautiously behind. Step by step we descended into complete darkness. I could hear the panting of my companion close behind. It was at this point a strange feeling came upon us, an unreal sensation. It was as if we were floating quite weightless, in a monstrous balloon. Then suddenly a loud explosion, a blinding flash of light, and we were plummeting down down down.

When I awoke, I still held the book in my hand. It was opened on the last page. I stared motionless for some minutes. The small ragged hole in the "D" in the END intrigued me; I hadn't noticed it before. I looked slowly round the room, trying to collect my tangled thoughts, "Was it all a dream," I wondered, expecting any second to be whisked away again. I pulled a spear-shaped thorn from the threads of my jacket, and my thoughts wandered back over the fantastic events of the past days, or was it weeks? Events so clear in every detail, that even now, I thought I could feel my hands and legs smarting from the ripping claws of the red gorse.

A loose page slipped from the book, and fell to the floor. I stooped to retrieve it; familiar words caught my eye: "Off with his head," "The Queen will be FURIOUS." I whispered the words aloud. Slowly the jigsaw began to fall into place.

The Old King must have wandered into the wrong book; surely that must be the answer. He was locked in a strange world, to which he could never belong, and couldn't escape. I searched feverishly until I found the book in which the old King really belonged. Perhaps I imagined I heard a faint sigh of relief as I replaced the lost page. I closed the book. As I looked at the picture of the old King on the shining cover, I saw a fleeting smile and a sly wink, but when I looked again, it was really just as it always had been.

I placed the two books on the table beside me, until I finally convinced myself that they were, and would always remain, two very ordinary books. My fantastic adventures were after all just a vivid dream. The sprig of red gorse I held in my fingers was, perhaps, pure coincidence.

My Beloved Country

Above the crown of the stately beech,
Blue skies, splashed with black of circling rooks,
The sun blinks through broad rakish wings,
That spill the air, with leisurely grace,
Harsh calls, discordant, yet in harmony,
With this peaceful land, unhurried place.

Where Summer smiles upon the earth, content,
T'will turn to shades of gold, when she is spent,
Ere' long, to touch the hand of Winter,
Who fashions her gown, of white, laced silver,
Soon the crocus will lift her golden head,
The snowdrop will spurt, from her silvery bed.

New life stirs again, in Natures breast,
Tender buds burst, where the birds will nest,
March winds give way, to April rain,
Then the world is refreshed, for 'tis Spring again,
Modest flowers of the field, look up t'ward the sun,
The earth grows warm, Summer smiles, 'tis done'.

For truly, it was in this place,
I heard the heart of England beat,
I felt her cool breath upon my cheek,
As she whispered softly, "Remember this,"
For I am yesterday".

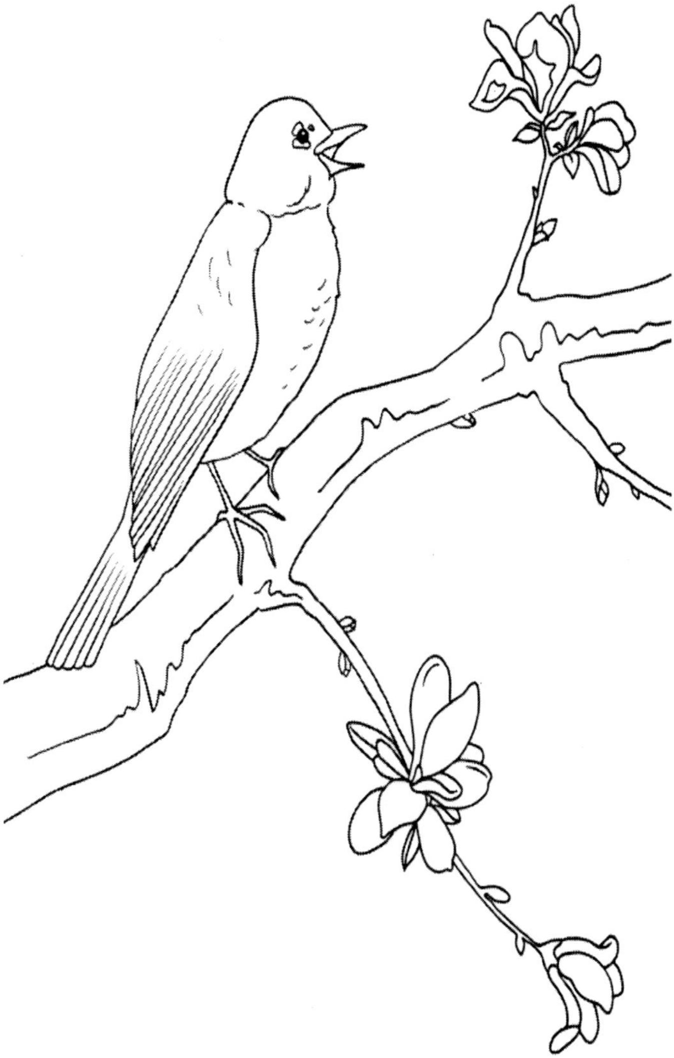

Childhood Memories.

I may turn at random, the pages of time,
Therein lies preserved, my conscious beginning,
Memories captured, by the eyes of childhood,
Aesthete observer of those colourful years,
Through you, I may wander again through tall spiked grass,
Waist high, bleached yellow, by the Summer sun,
I hear a world of music, from within.

Constant humming and strumming of dragon flies and bees,
Long horned grasshoppers, with musical wings,
Crickets that lead me such a merry dance,
Sound their shrill chirping concert nearby,
Yet the elusive performers, escape my detection,
As their chorus strums on from another direction.

The swallows are gathering, soon they will go,
Surging upwards and onwards, in search of the sun,
The cuckoo too leaves his borrowed nest,
To gorge and prepare for unaided flight.

Nests are deserted in the eaves of the ancient cot,
It's empty grey stone walls, are mossed and barnacled with snails,
Inside, the earthen floor, once some wild marshman trod,
To turn his kill on the spit in the open hearth.
The decayed remnants of the once stout door,

Rots and tilts, where the rats have gnawed.
Time has claimed, the land from the sea, and the man to dust,
The walls that once beheld these things, are silent,
The air is damp, it's icy chill, resentful,
Disturbed, by my intrusion,
I am glad to walk back into the sun.

Hovering so high, The Skylark pours forth silver song,
To the warmth of the sun that shines down,
To the wonders of the earth that look up,
His song, his farewell gift,
To the place of his birth, and the Summer.

A Moor hen bolts in sudden alarm,
From tall spiked reeds by the pond,
With her crimson blaze, and white flashed tail,
She skims the tall grass, and is gone.

The white collard mallard, donned Winter plumes,
He has done with his nest neath the pollarded willow,
Sweet sad willow, God's gentle tree,
Oft have I dreamed neath your slender boughs,
Whispering clouds tender green unfold,
To touch with grace, the swaying sedge,
The aged tree now leans, juts out from the waters edge
Silver Minnows dart through half bare roots,
Desperate fingers, that cling to softened earth,
The earth to her beloved child'

The soul of the dying tree, cries out,
Defying, the wind that means to bring about it's end,
When the head is bowed, and it can resist no more,
Then delicate leaves, that once billowed on the Summer air,
Are but silent tears that bleed on the fronded pool,
Then white vested frogs, will sleep on unconcerned,
In the damp hollowed earth that is left.

Racing Pigeon Ring: 65 P 379.

A tear unbidden, crept into the eye,
Of the boy who was watching, searching the sky,
He isn't with them, he's got to be there,
His fears were growing, but he wouldn't despair,

Watching in vain, all through that day,
And in fading light, till the sun slipped away,
He looked every day, but with hope finally gone,
The weeks relentlessly, drifted along,

He knew he's lose birds, but to the boy it came hard,
This one was special, his first precious card,

His legacy left, was a babe in the nest,
No doubt the experts can imagine the rest,
Yes, she won, was 3rd. Fed, 3000 birds,
To say the boy was delighted, are inadequate words,

Six months had passed by when he got in the stray,
With wing trailing down and feathers dull grey,
He stood on the loft, such a pitiful sight,
Not at all the sort that you would invite,
Into your loft, but he let him in,
Then rubbed the grime from his muddy ring,
He studied it closely to clearly define,
The figures stared back, it was '379'.

His heart filled with pity, but the incredible thing,
How had he lived and homed with that wing,
Hundreds of birds have come and gone,
But fate decreed, that just this one,
Should stay at home, and never race,
A sheltered perch, a well earned place,

Dispassionate advice, left no doubt,
When words 'Hard' and 'ruthless', were bandied about,
"It'll, get you nowhere, being soft,
You must carry no passengers in your loft",
Time proved the exception, the reward for compassion,
His youngsters more than provided, his meager rations,
Was this a luxury, he wasn't allowed,
To care for this bird, because he was proud,
Sentiment, perhaps, is a more honest word,
Butt somehow he isn't an ordinary bird,

Now the man Looks at the old un', his eyes kind in reflection

He can't be considered for Lerwick selection,
"I know you'd have flown it for me old mate",
Then he turns and walks on to a young candidate,

Oh! he still flies around, in a peculiar fashion,
but if the winds blowing strong, he doesn't go dashing,
around the loft, he just lets the suns rays,
Warm his old back, he just picks his days

Peg's Kingdom.

The old saddlers shop, with it's hollowed step,
Worn down by the feet of farming men,
Around the shabby door, on loops of string,
Hang fine leather straps for harnessing,

A man of the soil, in tough black boots,
Looks at the price of the leather and hopes,
The old harness he holds in his strong brown hand,
The saddler once more, will be able to mend.

Maybe this year if the harvest is good,
He could buy a fine bridle, with shiny brass studs,
Old Peg' ud look grand, in smart brasses and braids,
He could paint the old plough, and burnish the blades.

The harvest is in, there's still work to do,
There's bug Peg and the man, only the two,
Constant companions, ploughing the furrow,
The man talks to old Peg, of his dreams for the morrow.

Once more the harvest, barely pays for new seed,
"Sorry old girl, there's no bridle or braid,
Old Peg eats her oats, she doesn't mind,
Her stable is warm, her master is kind.

She can graze in the sun, there is no charge made,
Feel the strong hand gently stroking her head,
The sweet smell of the earth, the blue skies above,
These things are Peg's kingdom, with this man and his love.

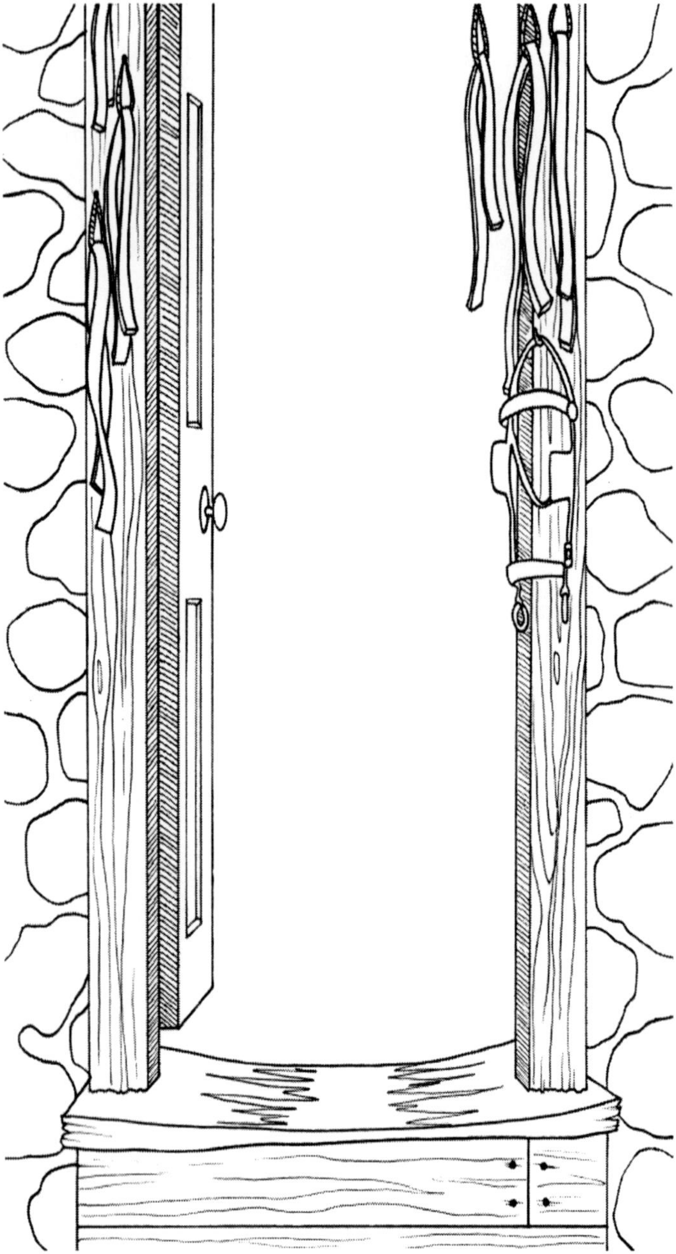

The Return Of Spring.

Have I not seen this place before,
When wrapped in winters white array,
When twisting shadows of leafless trees,
Cast long on the snow and crawled away,
Like skeleton hands toward waters edge,
To be devoured by reeds and frosted sedge.

The tranquil reflection of a snow thatched cot,
Was rippled in twain by a white collard duck,
Gliding silently by on the clear cold lake,
A crimson flash in the willow, told the robin was back.
The place is the same, it's beauty no less,
'Tis merely that Spring, again, has re-fashioned her dress.

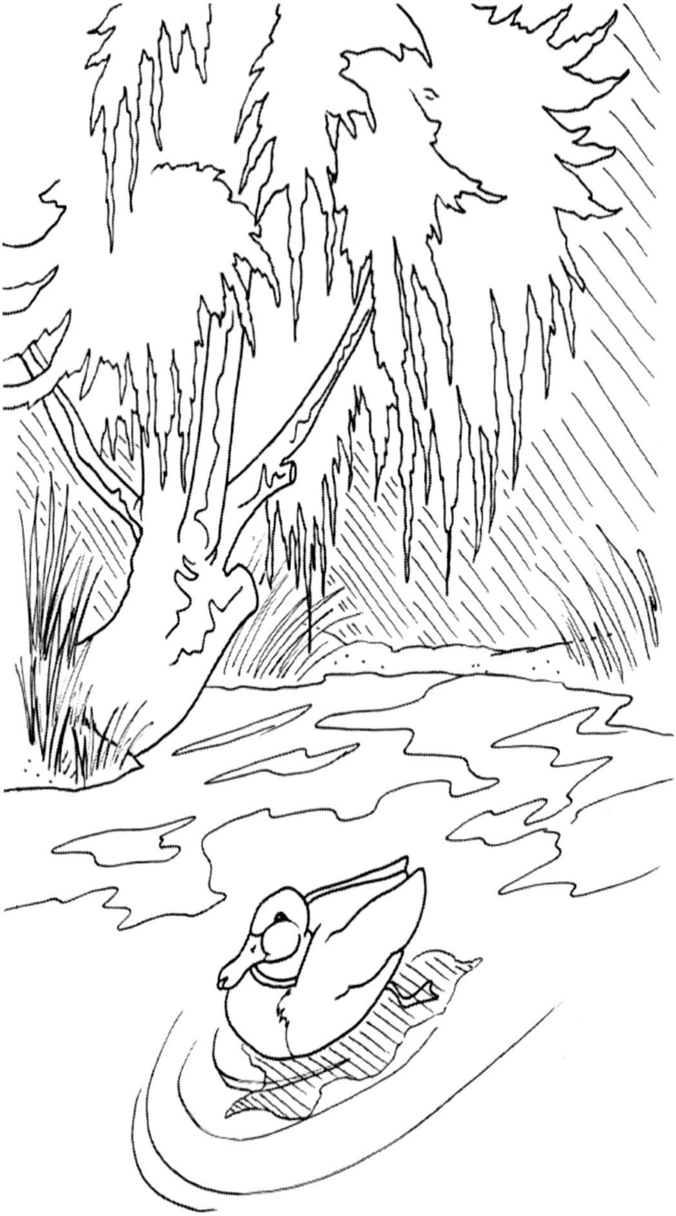

The Fenland Highwayman.

The villains face, with eyes that contemplate,

The lone traveler, who dares to ride the fens,
Where danger lurks, in the mist a hidden fate,
Twas here that Turpin brought ill gotten gains,
On which to realize,
Alas for him twas York bore witness,
To his own demise.

His life of robbing, rustling, plundering,
Like a swaggering dandy,
Hastened his own ending,

As ever, the would be hero,
When he leapt from the gibbet,
He departed this life, in a blaze of mad cap bravado.

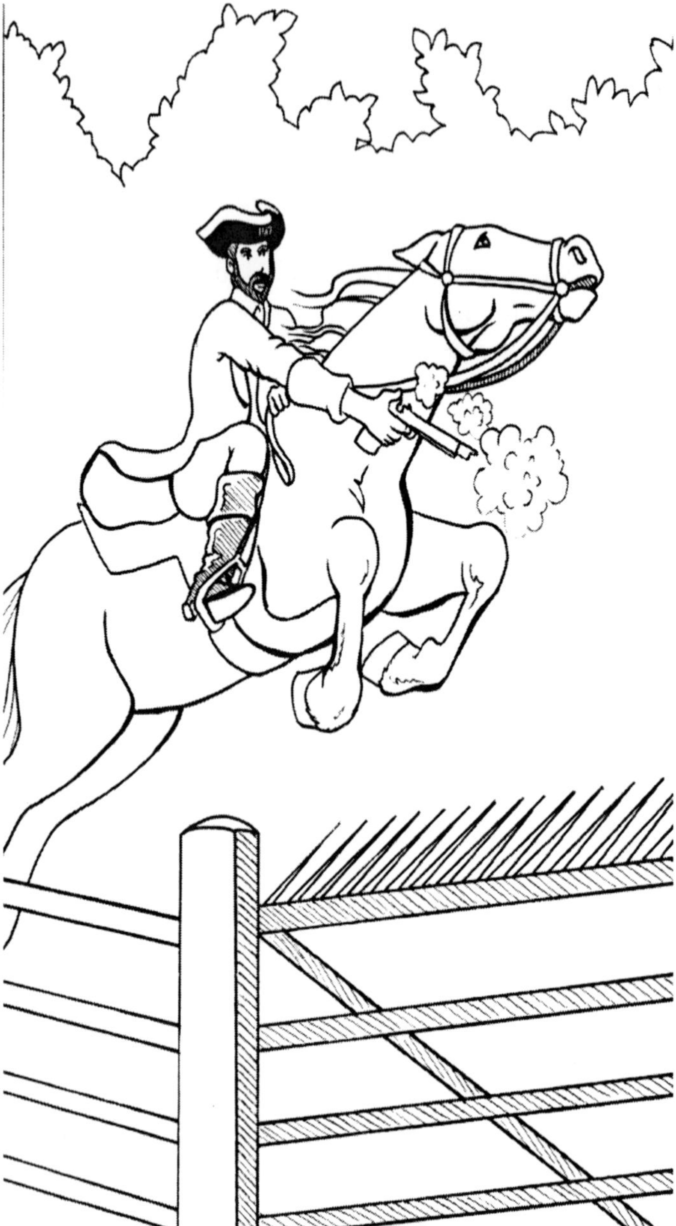

The Auction Of Sundries On The Cobblestones.

The bell rings out its familiar tones,
Calling folk to the auction on the cobblestones,
At 10 a. m. on Tuesday each week,
Folk gather round, a bargain to seek,
There are pitchforks and hoes and milking pails,
Rolls of wire, and tins of nails,
Some ploughing tackle, and a barely used spade,
That still bore the label, saying where it was made,
Looking sadly bizarre, a wrought iron bed,
Is picked up for eight bob, and a nod of the head,

A blacksmiths anvil, and smithying tools,
Made of fine hard steel, that had withstood the years,
That finally, wearied the man,
The glow of forge embers, on his sweated brow,
As he tempered the steel to repair an old plough,
A seventeen hand shire horse, waits to be shod,
For the village smithy, there was always a job.

A younger man stoops, to assess the tools worth,
And to see how they fit in his hand,
Then maybe he will purchase the memory,
Of his boyhood, his mentor, this man,
On those bygone days, he fondly reflects
And the small sad heap that lies in the dust,
Is all that is left, "just effects",

The sale is over for another day,
A life's work, like the crowd, drifts away.

Memory is the life you left behind,
The chain of shadows that spanned the years,
That rode the rolling tide.

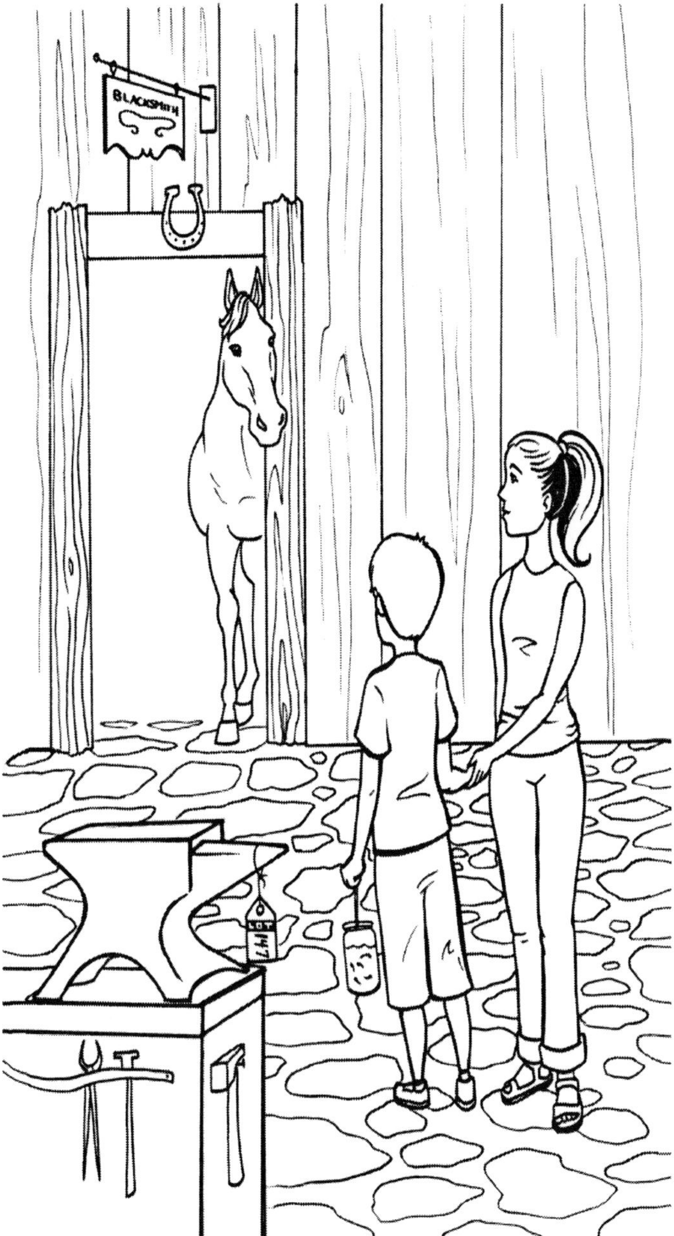
BLACKSMITH
LOT
147

Autumn Aquarelle.

The trees once more, abandon lifeless leaves,
Borne down by the breeze, to the water's edge,
Like tiny galleons, crisp and fragile,
They sweep and swirl, until caught in the sedge.

Beneath the still water, the pond is alive,
Small creatures abound, in their aquatic domain,
Twould seem unaware of the world without,
Yet should my image reflect, instantly vanish again.

They dart twixt stones and spidery plants,
That spurt from the mud, like ghostly hands,
They feign ne're to look, but always see,
I feel their pale round eyes, still watching me.

Cavorting newts, minnows, and hot tempered sticklebacks,
Hide neath quaint little crowfoot, and spreading frond,
A lily resplendent on her carpet of green,

Humble flowers pay homage, to their snow white Queen.

Young frogs bravely explore the muddy bank.
A brown warted toad strives to crouch undetected,
A stealthy hunter, has his presence betrayed,
When a startled moor-hen gives warning,
The stoat slides away.

The Windmill

Elegant silhouette in the evening sky,
Arms outstretched welcome the night,
Her work is done, the day spent well ,
The last sound spills down her weathered shell,

Her tiny windows glow golden rose,
Blinking back the setting sun,
Like a row of jewels, shining buttons,
To hold in place her long grey robe.

Soon night's cool hand will gently rest,
On earth still warm where the sun has blessed,
Then the hem of her gown grows undefined,
As evening mist its folds entwine,

Ere long the world sleeps at her feet,
Deep purple enfolds her starlit gown,
Her hands reach up to catch the moonbeams,
Silver threads, to be jewel her crown.

Thoughts of proud sentinels, on horizons line,
Still stir fond memories, of a childhood time,
There are fewer now who can I fear,
Feel those joys of yesteryear,
For the staff of life the wheat to grind,
What now, good servant of mankind,
Upon a time your aid was sought,
To drain the fens, now treat as naught,

Can we now you've done your duty,
Make no effort to preserve your beauty,

If only to repay the debt,
And in so doing, not forget,
Those joys of memory, now but few can share,
Who knew how it was because 'They were there'.

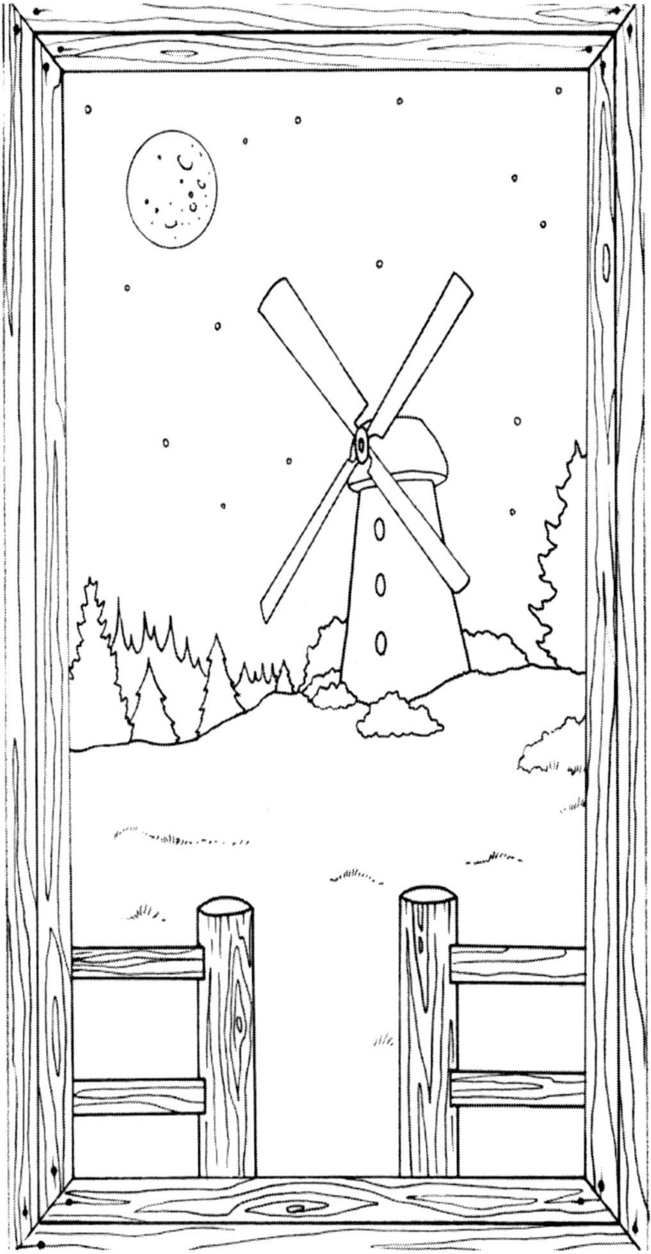

Yesterday

The blaring whistle of the oncoming train,
Pierces winters dawn and frosted pane,
The mighty engine, snorting power and steam,
Hauls laden coal and cattle trucks,
To the station yard, of the country town,
That stirs and wakes for market day.

Rosy cheeked children on their way to school,
run on to the footbridge, just to stand in the steam,
That belches through each grimy gap,
Beaming faces emerge, with damp mufflers and caps.

The buffers clang down the line of trucks,
The huge wheels scream protest biting steel and frost,
The fringe of ice from the wagon tops,
Slowly melts in the sun, slides down and drops.

The loud stomp of the hooves as the cattle stir,
Stiff from the journey, and cold night air,
One brown head bellows as they lumber round,
Through the cast iron vents, steams the shape of the sound.
Soon the cattle pens, that line the sides of the street,
Are filled with soft eyed, huge red timorous beast,
There are Lincoln Reds, and Large White Pigs,
Woolly sheep and chicken crates,

Rabbits and geese, all there to be sold,
At ten o'clock sharp the bell is tolled,
All interested parties respond to the sound,
The shrewd eyed buyers gather round,

First Lincoln Reds are singled out,
Led into the ring and turned about,
Midst the clang and crash of cast iron pens,
That shudder neath the weight of reluctant ones,

A brown smocked man in gaiters and boots,
Waves a gnarled old whopping stick,
His large red face bulges out and bawls,
Neath a battered tweed hat that looks far too small,
"Goo arn Gid up", accompanies innocuous clout,
At last the huge beast lumbers out,
To be weighed and sold, then herded back,
Slipping and sliding in the muck,

That splatters the pavement in front of shop doors,
From swollen gutters and sodden straw.

Still above the commotion of beast and man,
The auctioneer's voice just rattles on,
Unheeding the pig that makes good its escape,
Bolting through the Inn yard, the smocked man in its wake,
Darting and twisting the fugitive squeals,
Until finally cornered, is laid by the heels.

When the last beast is sold at the end of the day,
The water carts come to wash the muck away.
The auctioneer wearily, climbs down from his seat
Then children take over, for the game of the week,
"Lets pretend Auctions", when the youngest, somehow,
In spite of his protests, is always the cow,

Regardless, the game proceeds with a swing,
The small human cow is led in to the ring,
On to the weigher and up the ramp,
Where the unfortunate child is covered in stamps,
In bright yellow letters, saying "SOLD' to Bill Bloggs,
Portend painful discomfort, when being scrubbed off.

Too soon fading light, brings an end to the game,
The streets already, are sparkling with rhyme,

Folk melt away into the soft shadows of night,
That strangely divorce, the sound from the sight,
their steel studded boots still ring sharp and clear,
After the figures have disappeared.

Home to warm dumpling stews and firelight,
Behind comforting curtains, that close out cold night,
The lonely policeman stamps the cold from his feet,
As the snow starts to fall on the dark silent street.

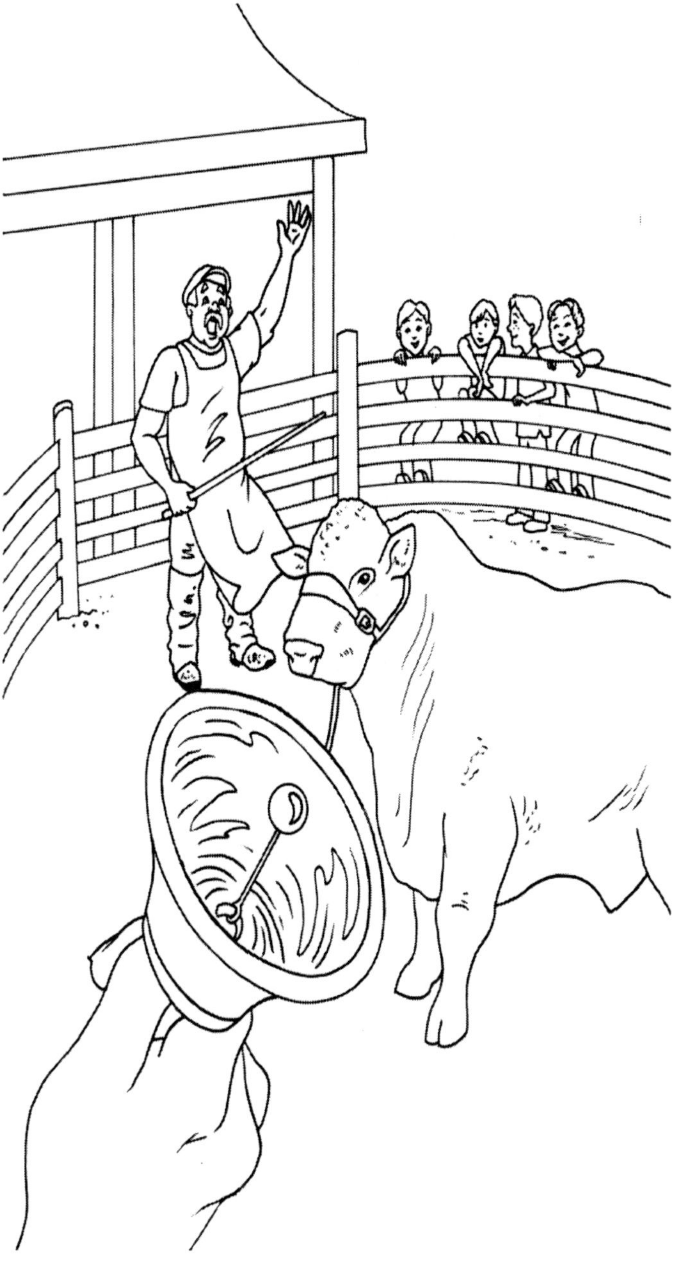

The Little Green Bus

Rattling through lanes, twixt fields of wheat,
Crawls the little green bus, with uncomfortable seats,
Bringing bonny brown ladies, with rose red cheeks,
To replenish their larders, perhaps buy a new hat,
Or a new piece of red striped coca mat.

They have discarded print bonnets and wellington boots,
To squeeze on tight shoes and volumous coats,
Huge hat pins for hats, that shade the sun from their eyes,
Trailing large leather bags, to bulge with supplies.

The bus gets so full, nearly touching the ground,
It started off square and finished up round,
The springs begin creaking, and the wheels are bumping,
It groans painfully on, like an oversized pumpkin.

There's Mrs Brown, undaunted by weather,
Frantically herding six children together,
Dear comical corpulent Joshua Dickens,
Clambers aboard, with a crate full of chickens.

The amply proportioned Mrs Blair,
Sweeps aboard with an arrogant air,
She arranges herself, on the lat two spare seats,
Baby Brown howls, because she's sat on his sweets.

Tucked in the corner, old Sam tries to doze,
With the feathers on Ms Blairs hat up his nose,

Daisy Bunn squeezes by with a tray full of pies,
Knocking said hat over Mrs Blair's eyes,
Off shoots a pie and splatters old Sam,
The unfortunate hat, now dripping plum jam.

When the little bus reaches it's destination
With a sigh off relief, it resolves it's inflation,
As it divests it's cargo, it wrinkles and kinks,
The distended shape perceptibly shrinks.

He shakes himself up, then puffs out his chest,
Standing with fine double deckers, and all the rest,

A smart bus looks down, with disdainful air,
"A Tin Lizzie', full of feathers and straw, I declare,"
Still as he watches and waits on the market place,
Our little green hero, keeps a smile on his face.

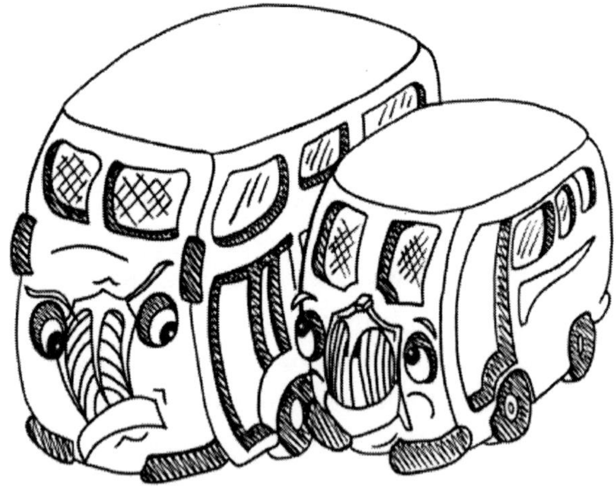

Beloved Island Home

Wild flowers of the field,
The song of the birds,
Are "Natures Gifts", inadequate words,

Green rolling hills,
We are free to roam,
To wander at our leisure,
This England, beloved island home,
A joy beyond all measure.

Warmed by the sun,
This emerald glade,
Sprinkled with buttercups,
There's no charge made.

Perchance one beautiful morning in May,
You will hear the Skylark singing,
Soaring high in clear blue sky,
As through the cloudless heaven he is winging.

In the field below, at the water hole,
A mare gently tends her new born foal,
For him the world is just beginning,
As he watches on this, his very first day,
Little Spring lambs skipping, enjoying their play,
Forsooth such sheer joys surround us, Hooray! Hooray!

The Bedevilled Moor

I glanced at my watch. The luminous dial glowed green in the fading daylight; it was almost 8:30 p.m. Already the warmth from the late September sun was vaporising into swirling mist across the open moorland. I shivered in the cooling air; not for the first time I secretly regretted our decision to take a touring and camping holiday so late in the year. This, I hasten to add, was not entirely from choice; alternative dates were somewhat limited, Steve and I being junior members in the employ of the respected Grayson and Grayson, Solicitors, where precedence for seniority on the revered holiday list is virtually sacrosanct.

Nevertheless, apart from this minor triviality I liked my work; there is something rather special for me in the old-fashioned book-lined offices. The three Grayson brothers, elderly, short, and somewhat portly in stature, were for me, strangely reminiscent of characters from Dickens. Each one sat in dignified opulence in his own carpeted office, behind an imposing polished oak desk, evoking an air of respectability, which reflected itself in their well-to-do clientele. I myself was a minor satellite of the senior partner, Mr Benjamin Grayson. As I thought of his genial, bespectacled face, podgy hands, and the shiny backside of his pinstriped trousers, I smiled to myself.

It was at this precise moment that the car engine spluttered ominously. In the fading light, Steve's knuckles gleamed white as he gripped the steering wheel. "Come on, old girl, you can't let us down, not here, for goodness' sake," Steve pleaded, but to no avail. The engine replied with two short unhealthy coughs, and the car lurched to a standstill. A moment of frustrated silence ensued, as we surveyed our predicament. "Better have a look, I suppose." Steve slid from his seat; he shivered as the cooling night air rushed in the open door. I reached for the torch and followed suit. Our fears were quickly realized. The already suspect coil had finally and irrevocably expired.

Having drawn the inevitable conclusion to our dilemma, we decided to light a fire. A bag of dry sticks, thoughtfully saved from our last camp, soon produced a crackling fire, and the prospect looked distinctly more cheerful. We returned to the car for our box of food, having decided to console ourselves further with mugs of hot soup, biscuits, and coffee.

It was from this moment onwards that events took a strange, disturbing turn. As we walked back to the fire, Steven stopped suddenly and gripped my arm. By the side of the fire, staring mournfully into the flames, sat a bizarre character, who by his attire could have stepped out of the Spanish court in the days of the Armada. Neither Steve or I spoke, or in fact could we; the incredibility of this ludicrous situation left us speechless. We approached slowly and with some trepidation, but our visitor seemed in no way surprised at our appearance. He rose to his feet, bowed low, and doffed his hat with that elegant style befitting his elaborate attire. Our complete bewilderment at this charade was understandable. After all, one would hardly expect to come upon a participant in a fancy dress ball on a mist-covered moor, at nightfall. After what seemed an interminable silence Steve spoke. The words jerked tightly from his dry lips. "Hello, old man, lost your way?" The unintended flippancy was delivered with none of his usual self-assurance, but the silence was broken. I started to breath again. As I walked to the fire, I held out my hand in greeting to our visitor. I was in no way surprised when my hand closed upon itself.

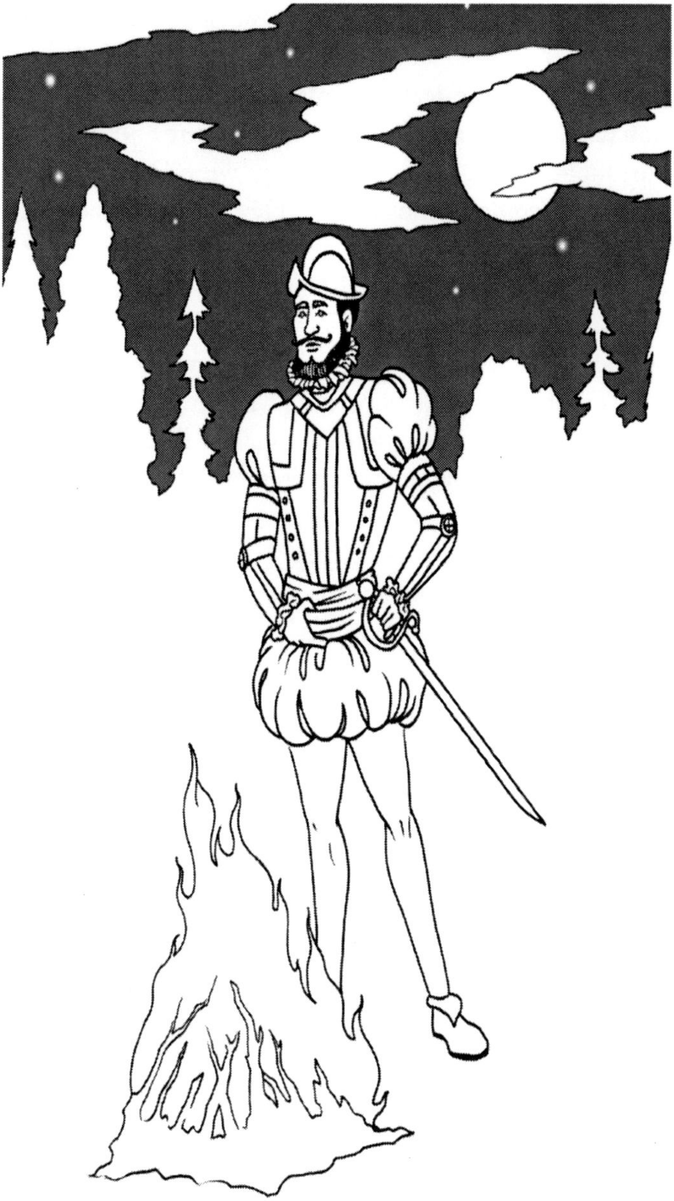

The little man bowed again, as he introduced himself as Manuel Carlos. His voice, like him, sounded weak and tired. He re-seated himself beside the fire, and watched as Steve and I replenished the fire and prepared our supper. This, out of courtesy, we offered to share with our nebulous companion. He declined, graciously. "Thank you, no. I really haven't anywhere to put it." His black eyes twinkled with mocking amusement. As we ourselves partook of the welcome sustenance, we listened to a strange account of what we presumed to be his past life and his subsequent reason for being here, His fascinating accent lent colour to the story. Only occasionally, in moments of excitement, did it become so pronounced, that he almost reverted to his native tongue. He unfolded a tale of political intrigues, of wicked men who sought by devious means to bring dishonour upon his house. His family, together with many unfortunate souls, were accused of heresy, and cruelly burnt at the stake. As he spoke these words, a chilling wind sprang up and moaned across the moorland. The fire spat and roared; the flames leapt skyward, casting weird cavorting shadows on the blanket of mist. Through the vicious devouring tongues of flame, I saw the face of a young woman, her mouth curled back from her teeth in terror. The scream of pain died on her lips; her head slumped forward, as the greedy flames spurted from her long dark hair. I swung round sharply. From somewhere out in the mist, across the moor called out brutal voices, screams of tortured souls. As the flames from the fire diminished, so the voices died away, and a quiet darkness fell. I could feel cold beads of perspiration on my forehead. I could just see Steve's white face in the misty darkness, "Let's get out of here," he whispered hoarsely. I fumbled blindly in the supply box for the torch, but its friendly light flung itself back from the blanket of fog that had swallowed the frightening frenzied shadows. What moments before had been a blazing inferno, was the cold remains of our supper and grey ashes of the fire. Alfonso had gone too.

Within moments we are hurrying in the direction of the road that edged the moor, hopefully back to civilisation and sanity. We never reached it! After walking for about ten minutes, I could barely see Steve a yard away, I felt alarmed. "Wait a minute, Steve, are we heading in the right direction?" I stooped and felt the ground, still wet moorland grass. Then we made the fatal mistake of trying to return to the car. With our bearings now completely gone, we wandered blindly. Each way we turned we were faced with an impenetrable blanket of fog. I took my blanket roll from my rucksack. There was nothing for it but to stay where we were, and wait till dawn. Trying not to fall asleep, we talked. At this point we felt that things could get no worse. How wrong we were. In less than fifteen minutes the temperature had plummeted, and we were enveloped in freezing fog. Was this an extension of the evil happenings on this bedevilled moor? Never before had I felt so cold. At first brief moments of wandering thoughts, then the severity of our plight began to lessen, to become almost acceptable. Was this succumbing to the inevitable? Deep down inside, a spark that refused to give way, then oblivion. I can't recall when any awareness returned, but very gradually my lucid moments lengthened, and my pretty nurse ceased in my confused mind to occasionally wear a velvet hat and don a short black beard. If it wasn't for Steve, to this day, I could not be certain where reality ended and illusion began. Steve told me that we owed a debt of gratitude to two backpackers, returning from a survival course on the moor, who gave us first aid and raised the alarm. It all seems so long ago now, lost in the mist of time. Steve still visits me. He is in the process of starting a solicitor's practice of his own now; we are looking forward to the day when I will be able to join him. They are very kind to me here. I am free to walk in the gardens, but the big gates with the iron bars close out the outside world. I feel so much better and feel sure I can take anything the outside world can throw at me.

Down And Out

The man climbed unsteadily up the cracked steps of the tatty lodging house. It was getting dark, and a blanket of November fog was falling rapidly. He reluctantly pulled his hand from the pocket of his shabby overcoat; his fingers stiff with cold, he groped for the dubious support of the rickety handrail. Reaching the top, he fumbled for the door handle. The door was locked. He stood, bemused and just a little inebriated, more from lack of food than overindulgence. Even the latter did little for the apprehension which he now felt, as he reached forward and timidly rapped the battered knocker, which clung desperately to the door by one loose screw. His fears were instantly confirmed, as a window above him was yanked up violently with a screech, and a peevish vehement voice spat, "If that's you, Foggarty, you can clear off, and quick or I'll call a copper." He lifted his eyes; through the swirling fog he could just see the tousled head of his landlady peering down, silhouetted against the dull light. She hesitated a second or two, to make sure it was Foggarty, before she renewed the attack, to pour abuse upon the unfortunate figure below. "Spent yer dole agen av yer? Well yer can buzz off, no rent no roof. I'm keeping yer baggage fer back rent." The window slammed down. Foggarty stood quite still for a moment. The faint light went out in the window above; he was quite alone. Any stimulating effects from his few drinks were gone too. At the best of times he was of slight stature; as he turned to descend the steps he seemed to shrink smaller than ever.

He wandered slowly; the street was deserted now. He crossed to the other side, where a few comforting lights shone faintly. "Hello, Sir, you alright?" The burly policeman who loomed out of the fog startled Foggarty. "Yes, yes," he assured him quickly, and scurried away. The terrifying thought of a vagrancy charge leapt into his mind. Whatever would his friends at the inn think? They were why he just had to have a few drinks each Friday, to keep up appearances. They were his only link with the past, where he could converse with fellows of his own kind. It was there that he could forget for a few hours that moment of lapse, fifteen years ago. The misappropriation of funds, the judge had called it. Years of humiliation and disgrace in prison. Hiding since then had presented no difficulties, as his family had disassociated themselves right from the very beginning. A odd friend or two had maintained contact for a short while; eventually there was no one. His vocation as a stockbroker ex-convict was unlikely to instil confidence in any prospective employer or customer. Consequently, idle hands for two years hadn't made things any easier. All these things from the past were tumbling in disjointed confusion in his mind. He became aware of his shoulder brushing against railings. He stopped, peered into an iron gateway: it was the park. He felt so tired; he would rest awhile. He sank wearily onto a bench, his eyelids heavy. He was so cold. He groped for the newspaper in his pocket, lay down and made pathetic attempts to cover himself, and from sheer exhaustion, fell asleep.

A sudden shaft of light pierced his fitful dreams. Half unconscious with cold, he thought he could hear a voice. It seemed so far away. His eyes opened very slowly. The voice was more distinct now. "Come along, sir, you can't sleep here." The policeman suspected something was wrong; his voice was kindly. "You need a bit of help, sir." In the darkness Fogarty felt the sting of tears.

It was several days before he realized fully that the white-coated figures he thought were figments of his imagination were real. He was being cared for with a kindness he had long since forgotten. A nurse placed a small package and a letter on his bed. "For you, Mr Foggarty." His unbelieving eyes surveyed them for a moment. "For me? There must be some mistake," he said, his voice a little tremulous. The nurse re-examined the name. "You are Mr Foggarty, aren't you?" His fingers, pale and thin, reached out for them. He opened the letter first. His eyes swept quickly to the foot of the page: "Yours sincerely, Richard Courtman." He began to read: "Dear Fogarty, So sorry to hear you haven't been well, we've missed you at the Inn. I am sending you a few ciggies along. By the way old chap, I have an interesting proposition, as soon as you are well enough. Advisory capacity, permanent, suit you down to the ground." The nurse pretended not to see Foggarty's hand brush swiftly across his eyes. He turned his head towards the window. The sun was shining; it was still winter, but everywhere felt warm, really warm.

Fisherman's Tale.

My ability as a fisherman was in no way professional, or for that matter accomplished; enthusiastically amateur I think is a fair assessment. I felt that I had progressed beyond "the one that got away" category and tried not to exaggerate the enormity of the ones that didn't. However, despite my efforts to establish the credibility of my "fishy stories", I still had to run the gauntlet of a barrage of ragging from my contemporaries at the office when I announced my intention to once again "do battle with the mighty seas." They made jocular remarks like "How's the sardine trade, Jonah?", "Bring us a whale back", or "The Two-ton Sprat, by Ivor Fish." In addition to this, the hazards of my intended vacation inevitably brought anxious prognostications from my well-meaning parents. Having survived this ordeal, I assured them of my constant awareness, and with my first flush of enthusiasm still surprisingly intact, I set off.

My journey to Glencove was uneventfully pleasant, particularly so as this was my third visit, so with fewer navigational problems, I was able to appreciate the scenery, which grew more and more beautiful. The soft undulations of the green fields became more pronounced, until the land dipped into deep valleys, then climbed into the hills until the tips were lost in the haze of the sun. Thin white lanes threaded their way to the humble abodes of lonely hill farmers, who tended their sheep on the sprawling slopes.

I continued to avoid the towns. Although by these deviations my journey was considerably prolonged, from an aesthetic point of view, it was infinitely preferable. The sun was warm and I was content to indulge myself in the intrinsic delights of the countryside, whilst contemplating my forthcoming adventure on the high seas, with my friend, Captain Abe Scott, retired.

On a steep down gradient the lane curved quite sharply to the right. I think only an inspired Shelley could hope to describe the culmination of beauty that lay at the foot of the hill. Savouring every moment, I drove slowly down. A local rustic, his brown cord trousers tied at the knees with string, plodded behind three large milking cows. He touched his battered cap with his stick, as I pulled over onto the grass verge to let him pass. I drove over a quaint stone bridge that spanned the stream, that glistened and bubbled around the stones in its shallow bed. It bulged and filled a pond, then carried on. In the reflection of weeping willows that fringed the pond, a row of tiny ducklings paddled frantically in their mother's wake.

The oak tree was in flower on the village green, amidst a cluster of grey stone cottages with diamond windowpanes. Further along, a sign with "TEAS" painted in neat black lettering, reminded me that I had not eaten since leaving home. I looked at my watch: 2:30 p.m., hardly teatime, but there was no harm in trying.

For a moment I stood with my hand on the tiny green gate, looking at the delightful white cottage with its thatched roof. Small shuttered windows and a trellised porch of climbing honeysuckle, the garden bright with hollyhocks, pansies, and forget-me-nots. As I walked towards the door of the tiny dwelling, I had the most ridiculous feeling that at any moment, the lid would lift up and it would turn out to be a music box: the door would open and a little doll lady in a lace cap, would dance jerkily round and round to the music, then disappear inside again; the lid could close and the music would stop.

When I knocked, the figure that opened the door was in fact bustling and bonny, with bright blue eyes that twinkled in her rosy tanned face. I hesitated a second, "I know it's a little early for tea but could you manage…" The little lady cut short my apology. "Come in, sir, come in, sit yourself down in the parlour." I stepped inside the doll's house; it was cool and pleasant. I was seated at a lace-covered table by a window that looked onto a paddock where light brown hens pecked hopefully at the sun-baked earth and little pink piglets were trying hard to get filthy, wallowing in a puddle by the drinking trough.

I readily accepted my hostess's offer of gammon, eggs, and mushrooms, followed by strawberries and cream. The bustling little lady disappeared into the kitchen, when what seemed like only seconds later, there was pandemonium and a flurry of feathers from the henhouse. She emerged with large brown eggs in a blue-and-white-striped bowl in one hand and a large stick in the other, with which she quickly subdued the aggressive attitude of a large Rhody Cockerel. A resounding "thwack" from the blackthorn staff and he decided to retire from the engagement, glaring belligerently from a safe distance.

Very soon, the delicious aroma of frying bacon wafted into the parlour. The room was small and quaint, furnished accordingly. A smaller-than-usual grandfather clock ticked steadily away in the corner; an aspidistra on a tall slender stand stood by the chintz-curtained windows.

Polished horse brasses and a priceless old lamp hung from a heavy dark oak beam that supported the ceiling. A Welsh dresser, lined with willow-patterned plates, with the inevitable china dogs in attendance. In soft melodious tones, the clock chimed at a quarter to three.

My attention was drawn to an antiquated gramophone, with a large brown horn. The atrocious quality of reproduction on such machines was not unknown to me, having suffered unavoidable pleasure on a previous occasion. At this moment my hostess appeared with a tray of sumptuous repast. I indicated the musical monstrosity and in a misguided attempt at polite conversation, enquired if it was still in working order, a remark I instantly regretted. "Oh yes, sir, it does indeed. Sir, would you loik some music woil you arve your tea?" Before I could decline, she pounced on the unfortunate machine, whirring the handle round and round so violently I quite expected disembodied springs, bits, and bobs would at any moment be flung to the four corners of the room. But the stalwart antiquity miraculously withstood the onslaught. Of course one could hardly expect a string quartet from the Ritz, but my digestive juices were hardly prepared for the rollicking medley from World War I.

In the middle of "Pack up your Troubles", the tenor voice descended slowly into a growl. My indefatigable hostess pounced again, rejuvenating the tired spring, but as the voice struggled slowly back up the scale, the needle stuck on "and smile … and smile … and smile." Privately, I was having hysterics in my strawberries and cream.

Having with considerable effort managed to control my amusement, I rose from my chair. "I must be on my way now. Thank you so much, the meal was delicious." The little lady, completely undaunted by her abortive attempts to provide a musical accompaniment during my meal, twinkled a smile. "Good-day Sir, do call again."

Refreshed by this amusing if not relaxing interlude, I resumed my journey. I had driven for two hours when a tang in the air told me I was nearing the sea and my eventual destination. It was exactly 5 p.m. when I knocked at the door of the pleasant home of Mr and Mrs Abe Scott. The pleasure of this reunion was a shared experience, as they greeted me most affably.

Having dispensed with the preliminary courtesies, which in this case included liberal portions of apple pie, chocolate cake, and large mugs of tea, we sat down to talk.

At one end of the parlour was a large bowed window that looked clear across the harbour. It was here that I had, in the past, learned more than a little of Abe Scott, this man of the sea, a trawler skipper for thirty years. I had listened engrossed as he brought to life moments of humour, drama, and disasters that had filled those years. Whilst taking into account the proverbial tendency to fanciful illusion that is said to accompany a seaman's yarn, Abe gave such credibility to his accounts that more than once, I would look towards the sea, and would well imagine it was happening at this very moment, and I myself was part of the drama. I was feeling the hypnotic fascination of this vast aquatic enigma of moods that creeps into the minds of strong hard men, feeding the imagination with fantasy of this mighty unconquerable ocean, one moment so clam and persuasive, the next wild and crashing with anger.

It was on the ninth day of my holiday that events took a somewhat unusual turn for me. Capt. Abe had hired a small coastal craft for me for the day. I sailed north, about half a mile off shore. The sun was warm, and in a freshening breeze, the visibility was perfect. I passed small bays where dilapidated remnants of small fishing craft where the only reminder of those bygone days, and a way of life that had been overtaken by commerce. The young had moved onto pastures new; only the elderly remained to reflect on the bygones.

Now imposing villas recline in solitary opulence, with equally impressive sailing craft moored alongside. Safely detached, shrieks of delight from bathers splashing and diving into the waves throwing huge beach balls, or whacking smaller ones with cricket bats. All in all, a community bent on enjoying this glorious day.

A few miles further along the coast, the coastline hardened, until the jagged points of huge cliffs loomed and stabbed ominously skyward. It was then that the engine coughed, then settled back into its rhythm for a moment, and then a series of ominous coughs and splutters caused me concern. I was not more than a mile off shore, but my attempts to re-liven the engine had no effect, so I steered the boat shorewards. Without more ado she finally spluttered and stopped. I grabbed the mooring rope, waded to the beach, and lashed her to a large pinnacle of rock firmly embedded in the stony beach. Having done this, I looked about me and surveyed the situation. I had very little choice, other than to scale the cliff at the most accessible point, to see what lay beyond. At this point the cliffs dipped quite sharply. Obviously at some time, part of it had fallen. I threaded my way up the stony beach, round huge boulders and lonely pools deserted by the tide. The peaks glowed with the gold of the setting sun, the dark shadows of the cliffs sprawled over the stones, and slid silently into the sea.

I stood and considered my plight. The dubious qualification of having once proudly acquired my Boy Scouts Rock Climbing Badge did little to comfort me. In fact, reflecting upon this inadequacy merely caused cold beads of perspiration to spurt from my brow. The fall of rock at the foot of the cliff, made the start of my climb comparatively easy; the remaining part presented a more daunting task. I reached for a handhold; the climb had begun. The first fifteen feet were, to say the least, precarious. After this the face sloped; thus gravity assisted a little. From thereon I reached the peak, triumphant, and not a little relieved.

I turned and looked down from where I stood. A veritable mountain of disgorged cliff and huge boulders were strewn 100 yards down into the valley. Bright green fields sprawled away down to converge on a huddle of tiny roofs of cottages and the grey spire of a village church. It was as though the weight of the little village had sunk a hollow, in a huge green velvet cushion, patterned with a network of grey stone walls that seemed to wander aimlessly on, yet cross and meet with artistic precision. I started to descend, cautiously, I had an uneasy feeling that the steep decline of rocks was more than a little insecure. This profound prognostication was suddenly and dramatically confirmed when the rocks beneath my feet began to move.

The next moment I was hurtling down the mountain of stone. The world began to spin faster and faster. I was vaguely aware of rocks crashing and careering past me. I remembered no more. When I opened my eyes slowly and thankfully, I became aware that I was at least still alive. Having established this fact, I lifted my hand and painfully explored the large lump on my cranium. I suppose it is to be expected that I couldn't escape the ordeal completely unscathed; both my knees were bleeding. I decided to seek help from the occupant of a small dwelling tucked under the overhang of the cliff, consequently not visible from my first vantage point. The door was open. I knocked, but no one answered. I could see a sparsely furnished room. At a scrubbed top table sat a young woman with long golden hair that waved and fell about the shoulders of her pale grey dress. She was absorbed in her writing, and obviously did not wish to be disturbed. So not wanting to intrude further, I went to a water pump in the field and washed the abrasions on my knees. The ice cold water soon stopped the bleeding, and I set off down the emerald gradient to the village. I was soon aware of the curious glances at me, the stranger in the midst, but I put them more at ease when I related my story. My priority was to find some accommodation, and get to a telephone to ring Abe Scott, to decide the quickest way to get myself and the boat back to base. There was no hotel, but a Mr and Mrs Murray kindly offered me lodgings until I could arrange my return. I told them my story, but when I got to the point where I went to the cottage, and saw the young woman writing at the table but who didn't answer the door, Mr Murray said, "But no one lives there anymore." He then proceeded to enlighten me on the history of the cottage, probably to quieten the look of disbelief on my countenance.

"Some time ago, there was a young couple who wed, and built their home at the foot of the cliffs, Robbie and Jenny Grey. They were both writers, authors of some standing, I believe. Then disaster struck; after a long spell of strong wind and torrential rain, without warning part of the cliff broke away, and came crashing down, Robbie was killed; he wasn't found for several days. Jenny died six months later, of a broken heart they say. Some manuscripts were found in the cottage. They are in the rector's keeping; ask him if you could see them. Since then two families have occupied the cottage briefly, but both have left. They felt a presence, not at all menacing or threatening, an air of melancholy, which persisted." To say I found this account somewhat disturbing is an understatement, but first things first, I spoke to Abe on the phone. He would hire a craft and bring her and an old buddy, an "engine boffin", to the harbour, back along the coast, where the holiday makers revelled. They would pick me up, and hopefully the boat's reluctant engine would not present too much of a problem Then thank goodness it will be back to the Scotts' pleasant home. There was no difficulty with transport back to the harbour, the long sandy beach, and all that it offered here. I confess I had to see the manuscripts that were found in the cottage. The next day I went to see the rector, told him of my experience, and asked to see them. He produced a folder which contained one or two short stories, but in addition there were one or two personal poems which portrayed the wonderful devotion of the two writers.

> We built our home
> Neathe the tall grey peaks,
> Where the valley so green,
> Rolls away from our feet,
> We tend to our sheep,
> Watch the spring lambs play,
> How happy we are
> My sweet Jenny Grey.

> I still see the smile in my Robbie's eyes,
> Yet I know not where my true love lies,
> The crumbling peak would never tell
> Twas beneath the stone, my Robbie fell.

Other than having confirmed Mr Murray's account of the previous tragedy at the cottage, my perusal of the documents did nothing to clarify the inexplicable events. I phoned Abe and made final arrangements for the following morning. I was determined not to dwell on the mystery, but to enjoy the last few days of my holiday, which began with a pleasant journey back to the Scotts, incidentally with Abe, in the boat that had caused the catalogue of events.

Abe's buddy had quickly solved the engine problem, and ferried the other boat. We arrived home at 5 p.m. to a concerned Mrs Scott, anxious to hear all about the mishap. After tea we sat down at the bay window. For once, I had a story to tell, which they listened to intently, and agreed with me not to dwell upon the happenings at the cottage. There was no answer. Abe made the last few days of my holiday especially enjoyable, with the boat and fishing trips. Then came my return home. I called at the little cottage for sustenance and renewed my acquaintance with the pleasant little hostess. Then it was back to normality at home and the office. I did not tell them of the cottage episode, but impressed upon them what a remarkable holiday it was.

The Candy Floss Caper

The morning sun shone through the window, onto the tousled head of the boy. Just a crown of damp brown curls, visible over the sheets. One blue eye slowly emerged from the depths and blinked into the sunlight. Perched high in the branches of the tall tree was the blackbird, bursting with song, but ever watchful of his territory, his coal-black shape featureless against the sun, and the clear blue sky.

The boy watched the etchings of silver frost on the window panes, slowly melt in the winter sun and slide down. There was a cold sharpness in the air, but his reluctance to leave the warmth and comfort of his bed disappeared when he remembered it was Saturday. He leapt out of bed and dressed quickly, complete with cap, muffler and gloves. He paused thoughtfully at the bathroom door, opened it; then turning the taps on full, he proceeded to give a remarkable impression of vigorous activity, adding the final touches with a little tuneless whistling, suitably muffled by the towel. Mum's voice from the doorway, brought the sound effects to an abrupt conclusion, and he emerged from the towel with a red-faced giggle. "Now my lad, how about a proper wash-off with that coat," chided Mum, turning quickly away to hide her smile,. "And don' t forget to clean those teeth," she called, as she descended the stairs. He peeled off his coat with reluctance, but the thought of football spurred him on, and having survived the ordeal, he bounded down the stairs. "No time for brekkers Mum, going to watch the football match." He swept through the kitchen before Mum could raise any objection. She shook her head and smiled as she watched the sturdy little figure speed down the garden path, then up the long hill that led to the town. So he had to pass the cottage of the old witch, who had a distinct aversion to small boys, and often chased them off with her broom. There were stories told in frightened whispers that she had actually been seen on a broomstick, speeding along in the darkness, casting spells. Furthermore, Trudy Brooks was convinced that the witch's scrawny cat, with its large yellow eyes, was really a handsome prince that had fallen foul of the witch. Whilst Nellie Bloggs conveniently turned the unfortunate embarrassment of her spotty face into a moment of glory, when she claimed that her affliction was in fact the result of the witch's revenge, having once, in a moment of bravado, poked her tongue out at the old woman.

The boy glanced furtively at the window of the cottage Yes, there she was, with the same squeezed lemon look that he was sure could turn candy floss into acid drops in a twinkling. Ah, candy floss! He licked his lips in anticipation. His fingers groped instinctively, through the grubby tangle of conker strings and rubber bands, to the bottom of his pocket, from which he eventually retrieved the elusive one pound coin. He quickened his step, and rounded the corner to Mrs Day's shop. He peered through the small panes of the window at small dishes of gobstoppers, jap desserts, aniseed balls, long liquorice shoelaces, tiger nuts, and sherbet dips. He opened the door sharply to make the bell above clang louder, and watched it bobbing up and down on its spring. The shop felt warm and cosy, with the delicious smell of spices, new bread, pear drops, and bundles of creosoted kindling. The sound of the bell had hardly died away, when Mrs Day appeared silently from the back room. "Candy floss please, Mrs Day." The boy ,with a confident flourish, slapped the clinking coin onto the sloping sides of the money dish, until he was handed a monstrous pink cloud on a stick. He moistened his lips in anticipation, and turned his head at various angles to determine the best direction of attack. He emerged from the first sortie quite well, only a small pile on each cheek, and one on the tip of his nose, to mark the engagement.

He crossed the road to the park his candy floss, "licked into shape", became a handsome charger; now it was his Olympic Torch. He raised it triumphantly above his head, running on and on, with the sound of thousands cheering, He ran his lap of honour, round the football pitch, he mounted the steps of the stand for the grand finale. With a sweeping flourish, he set alight the Olympic Flame, and in his loudest grownup voice, proclaimed, "Let the Games Begin."

He perched himself precariously on the top of the shiny handrail, and began to slide quickly to the bottom. His spectacular descent was momentarily interrupted by Mr Bloggs, who unfortunately turned his head at the wrong second, and his vision was obliterated by a wide streak of candy floss deposited across his spectacles. The people around roared with laughter, but Mr Bloggs was simply furious. The boy disappeared quickly into the crowd. He wormed his way to the front of the huddled spectators, who, with hands thrust deep into their pockets, stood stamping their feet to keep warm waiting for the game to begin.

A cheer went up as the visiting team appeared, then a louder one for the "Boys in Blue". Local enthusiasts sounded rattles and waved bobble hats and scarves.

The whistle blew and the game began.

The boy's aspirations for world fame in the Olympics were immediately forgotten. His blue eyes peered over the top of his candy floss at the skill of the players in their striped socks and bright blue shirts. The challengers wore red. With the tip of his tongue he slowly dislodged tiny fragments of floss, making it last as long as possible.

He glanced down for just a second. Then it happened. The world exploded around him, and he reeled over backwards, gasping. The telltale blobs of candy floss on the muddy ball at his elbow told the sad, sad story. Two tiny watery eyes blinked out of the floss, and ruefully surveyed the empty stick, clutched in one hand, whilst the other gingerly explored his already swelling proboscis.

The anxious ring of faces peering down slowly relaxed into smiles, as the boy's face, surrounded by a fluffy pink beard, split into a watery grin. His nose had already taken on a glorious rosy hue. "Well, I do declare, it's Santa Claus, 'in the pink'," joked one wag. Everyone laughed, and the boy giggled, just a wee bit tearfully. Someone produced the first aid sponge, and wiped away the muddy floss. The young man smiled as the cherubic face emerged. "Right y'arr laddies, orn with the game," called the man in the blue track suit. "Come over here laddie, sut yersel doon by me." He held out a shiny new one pound coin to the boy. "Och aye you're a breeve wee lad, bay yersel anither carndie." The boy smiled and tucked the coin safely away in his pocket. The players ran back on to the pitch, and feeling quite important, the boy seated himself on the bench, marked in large white letters, For Officials Only.

The game continued, and the excitement mounted.

The man's accent grew broader by the minute, as he bawled frantic instructions to inspire his players. The boy watched fascinated, unconsciously mouthing the words and elastic facial contortions of the man, as he produced an unintelligible tirade of dialogue, which by some incredible magic, brought the required response from the players. These verbal outbursts were accompanied by much weaving and bobbing and waving of arms. These somewhat overzealous gesticulations caused his already florid complexion to grow redder and redder. Ten minutes to go and the score was 1-1; then a tremendous shot from 25 yards put the home team ahead. When the final whistle blew, it was victory for the boys in blue. The man patted the boy on the head, saying "Ye brot us luck, laddie." Then he bounded off to greet the players with "Well done, lads." The players smiled back. Their smart strip was now splattered with mud, and their hot breath billowed on the cold air as they ran. The boy jumped down from the bench, and watched until the last player had disappeared into the dressing room; then he turned and made his way across the park.

Dreaming of the day when he would be a famous footballer, he picked up and dribbled an empty tea carton. He placed it carefully in front of the goalmouth, backed away, then charged and took a mighty kick, missed, slipped, and was momentarily airborne before landing with a squelch in the quagmire. As he scraped the cakes of mud off his knees, he glanced furtively from side to side, but the last few stragglers were hurrying towards the gate. The humour of the situation having obviously escaped the boy, he stamped ferociously on the carton and squashed it flat, then quickly followed the others out of the gate and into the town.

He stopped, as was his habit, at the window of the sports shop, to look at the brightly coloured shirts, striped socks, and bobble hats, but very especially at the shiny black football boots with white leather trim. He thoughtfully fingered the one pound coin in his pocket, but even his youthful optimism failed to bridge the yawning gap between this and the £39 99*d* tag attached to the boots.

Any hope of parental generosity faded away when he dismally surveyed his mud-caked coat and shoes. Even by his own boyish standards, he looked a mess. He turned thoughtfully away and made for home. Even the huge conkers he found under the horse chestnut tree failed to console him, or take his mind off those shiny black boots. He reached his home, but before he went in, he tried, in desperation, to rub the mud from his coat, but only succeeded in spreading it further. The effect of this was soon apparent. By the look of utter dismay on Mum's face, as she stared in disbelief at the muddy, red-nosed little figure before her.

After the inevitable motherly remonstrations, the boy was ordered to a steaming hot bath, and told to hurry as lunch was nearly ready. He needed little persuasion, having savoured the mouth-watering aroma from the stewpot whilst being "ticked off" in a remarkably short time. He was sampling the stew with great relish, but owing to prevailing circumstances, kept a suitably subdued expression on his clean rosy face.

Lunch was finished, and his father sat silently behind his newspaper. Mum was clanging the lunch pots a little louder than usual, so still feeling distinctly unpopular didn't make it easy for the boy to broach the subject of football boots. He took a deep breath, then in a tight hollow little voice, said, "I'm saving up for some football boots." He stared hopefully at the back of his father's paper. There was no response, and his confidence ebbed. Then his father slowly lowered the paper, and a smile crept into his eyes as he looked at the small, apprehensive, red-nosed repentant at the table. "By the look of things you could do with some boxing gloves." The boy giggled, and cupped his hand over his red nose. "The football did it," he chortled.

But the man gave me this look." He fumbled hurriedly for the pound coin and displayed it proudly. "It's for some boots." His father laughed, "It seems a painful way to earn a pair of boots, lad." He looked at the eager face of his son and remembered when he was young himself. Times were hard in those days, and work for his father not easily come by. With four boys in the family, boots for school were almost a luxury, and new football boots were not a priority, but times had changed, rightly so. His blue eyes twinkled with amusement as he listened to the boy as he described the happenings of the day, being a little cautious at one point, as he feared that what happened to Mr Bloggs might be his undoing. So with childlike philosophy, he put the unfortunate episode into a more acceptable nutshell.

By saying "Mr Bloggs didn't know it was me, cos he couldn't see," this delightful reassurance brought a smile to his father's face, and his resistance finally crumbled. He reached for his savings tin from the cupboard. "Come along then, son, let us see what we can do." Needless to say, the boy needed no second bidding, and they were soon on their way to town. They walked briskly in the cold air, the small boy stretching, as he tried to match stride for stride with his father's long legs. The wind was strong and biting cold; the large snowflakes that began to fall were swept up and sent swirling and stinging into their faces. It was indeed a relief to get inside the warm shop. They were greeted by a plumpish man with a broad beaming face that culminated in a gleaming dome-shaped cranium, edged with a fringe of spiky hair that stabbed outwards. "Have you any football boots to fit the boy, size *eleven* I believe?" his Father enquired. "Yes sir, size eleven, here we are sir." The man placed two shiny black boots trimmed with white leather on the counter. "Are these the ones, son?" He beamed at the boy, who nodded eagerly as he instinctively ran his hand over the boots. He tied the laces together and hung the boots round his neck, like the big boys at school. He looked up, his eyes bright with excitement. His Father smiled. "We'd better take some shorts and a shirt too, please." Then he took two blue-and-white-striped bobble hats from the stand and plonked one on the boy's head and one on his own. "I think I'd better come with you next week, sonny boy," he joked. The boy squirmed with delight. What with presents and the large fluffy snowflakes clinging to the window, it just seemed like Christmas.

His elation was, however, temporarily suspended; at that precise moment, the door opened and in walked Mr Bloggs. The boy went crimson; his skin began to prickle. "Good afternoon, Ernie," his father greeted Mr Bloggs with amiable composure. "Not a very good one, I'm afraid," returned Bloggs, then he turned to the boy. "You've got a good colour, lad." The boy's eyes darted from Bloggs to his father and black to Bloggs. "Did you enjoy the match today, young fellow?" Bloggs persisted. The boy managed a sickly little smile on his guilt-ridden countenance, and he nodded his head in reply.

Obviously finding this conversation a trifle negative, Mr Bloggs gave a little grunt and turned to the counter to be served, and the heat was off. By this time the salesman had packed the parcel, and wishing him good day, they stepped out into what was now almost a blizzard. The snow was falling faster than ever, and the boy pulled his hat over his ears. Clutching his precious parcel, he took his father's hand, and they hurried homewards. It was good to be home; they quickly stamped the snow from their shoes and closed the door on blinding snow. The fire was burning brightly; everything looked warm and cosy. On the table were hot buttered crumpets, teacakes, and homemade jam. Mum was highly amused at the snow-covered bobble hats. "You spoil the boy," she said kindly. Then she readily shared in the excitement as she hastily tore open the paper parcel to display its treasured contents. She gave the boy a hug. "They're lovely. Now you must try them on." After a brief preoccupation with the delicious crumpets and teacakes, he dressed in his full regalia, bobble hat and all. Then he trotted into the room, to the tumultuous applause of both parents. He proceeded to give a somewhat overambitious demonstration of flashy footwork. Fortunately no harm was done; his father caught him before he hit the floor. He sprawled with tangled legs into his father's arms, helpless with laughter. The highlights of the day's soccer came on the television. He squatted down to watch the masters, savouring to the last moment this remarkable day. Inevitably the warmth of the room, and the hectic excitement, began to tell. His eyelids grew heavy; it was the signal for bed. He was nearly too tired to enjoy his piggyback ride up the stairs. The cold air in the bedroom revived him temporarily, and he quickly got into his pyjamas. Still wearing his bobble hat, he jumped into bed, carefully placing his precious boots beside his pillow. He put out the light. The brilliance of the moon and stars was already dimmed by a newly-formed film of frosted lace upon the windowpanes. In the darkness, he drew the boots closer. He loved the strong rich smell of the new leather. He slid further down into the warmth and comfort of his bed, and with his eyelids slowly closing, came that moment when his thoughts of today slip quietly into his hopes for tomorrow. In between he could dream that he was Ryan Giggs and David Beckham all rolled into one, and after all, who knows?